Cricket Witness:

Whites On Green

A history of cricket at St. Helen's, Swansea

Andrew Hignell & Bob Harragan

Dedication

In memory of Bob, Harvey and Alcwyn

First published in Great Britain by
Association of Cricket Statisticians and Historians
Bedford MK40 4FG.

British Library Cataloguing-in-Publication Data.
A catalogue record for this book is available from the British Library.

ISBN: 978 1 912421 00 8
Typeset and printed by The City Press Leeds Ltd

Contents

Preface

The idea for this book, the fifth in the Cricket Witness series, celebrating some of the finest moments in the history of the St. Helen's cricket ground in Swansea, belonged to Bob Harragan. Having heard about the series, he first approached the Association during the summer 2015 and, after several telephone conversations, he subsequently forwarded, an initial manuscript besides suggesting areas we could work on in collaboration on a book celebrating the rich history of a ground whose future as a long-term venue for county cricket has been in doubt for several years.

Sadly, Bob's health deteriorated later that year and he passed away in hospital in Llanelli on 26 January, 2016. Our joint efforts on this book were still very much in their infancy but, as someone who shared his passion for the ground overlooking the Severn Estuary, I was keen that his painstaking research efforts on behalf of the ACS saw fruition. During the course of the last couple of years, I have therefore attempted to fill in the gaps and round off what I hope is a fitting tribute to someone who spent many years delving into the fascinating early history of cricket in South Wales.

Born in Romford in 1954, Bob had worked as a sports journalist in West Wales from 1973, chiefly with the *Llanelli Star* newspaper. He was also the manager of the Carmarthenshire Under 11s, a committee member of the South Wales Junior Cricket League and Honorary Statistician for the Welsh Schools Cricket Association. He also held a record-keeping role with the Welsh national side which, under the management of the Welsh Cricket Association, took part in the Triple Crown competition from the early 1970s.

Bob also wrote several sports books, including the highly acclaimed *"History of Llanelli Cricket Club"* in 1991 and "Images of Wales - Llanelli RFC" in 1997. If Llanelli was his place of work, Stradey Park was his sporting base, Swansea was most definitely his next favourite ground and whether it was a county fixture, Minor County match, club game or a contest involving juniors, Bob would go out of his way to be present, ensuring that the efforts of the county professional, international stars, club members or young boys did not go unrecorded. Fittingly, some of the proceeds from the sale of this book are going to the Cricket in Wales Foundation Trust, set up by Cricket Wales and Glamorgan CCC to nurture grassroots cricket.

Andrew Hignell

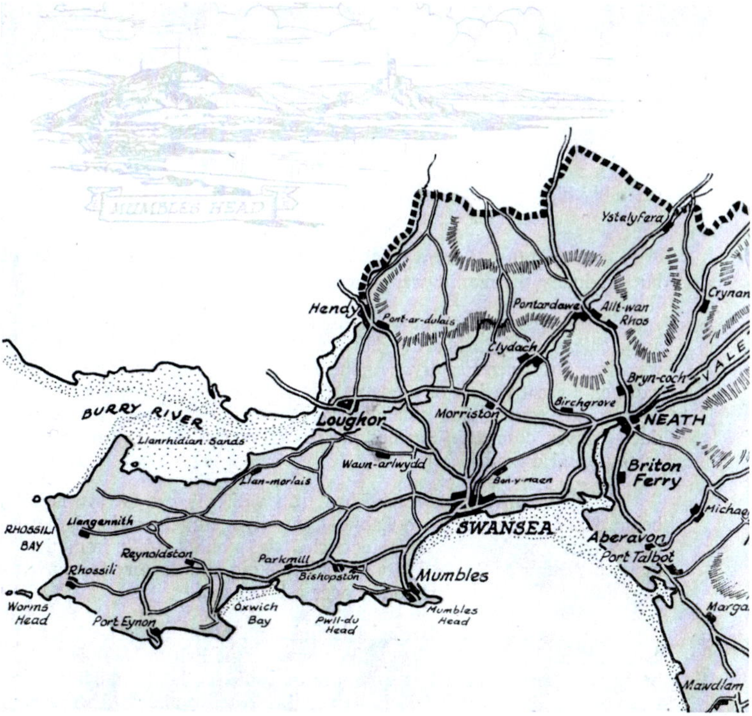

Swansea and its environs, taken from the Glamorgan County Review, *published by the Glamorgan County Council in 1950.*

Introduction by Bob Harragan

It's the only first-class ground in the United Kingdom where you can see the sea – the St. Helen's ground in Swansea where some of the most memorable days in Glamorgan's history have thrilled the crowds shoe-horned into the tiered enclosures that lined the boundaries at one of county cricket's most idiosyncratic venues.

The ebb and flow of the tide in Swansea Bay have even influenced the decisions by the Glamorgan captains on winning the toss to either bat or bowl, with an incoming tide frequently assisting the bowlers set to perform on the wicket which was created during the Victorian era on a series of reclaimed sandbanks adjacent to the shoreline road leading to the Mumbles.

Indeed, it was at the St. Helens ground where Glamorgan secured a dramatic two-day victory over the 1951 Springboks, where the guile and spin of Johnnie Clay confounded Australian batting legend Don Bradman, where Glamorgan defeated the Australians on successive tours in 1964 and 1968, and where during the latter season Garry Sobers became the first man in cricket history to hit six sixes in an over.

It was the ground where in the late 1940s, John Arlott sat in the BBC Radio commentary box, alongside Swansea's favourite son, Dylan Thomas, and where in 1976 West Indian legend Clive Lloyd struck the world's fastest double-hundred. It's a ground which also witnessed the astonishing debut hundred by Matthew Maynard in 1985, as well as some remarkable bowling by Jim Pressdee and Don Shepherd during the Championship match against Yorkshire in 1965 with each spinner taking nine wickets in an innings.

The unique maritime microclimate at St. Helen's has also favoured the swing bowlers with Lincolnshire defeating Glamorgan in their Gillette Cup encounter in 1974 after winning the toss and putting the first-class county in to bat. This book recalls a selection of these great and remarkable days in the history of the St. Helen's ground, as well as outlining the events in the Victorian era which led to the creation of the ground in the first place.

An aerial view of the St. Helen's rugby and cricket ground, plus the areas of housing which, if the Corporation had won sway over the town's sportsmen, would have engulfed this most unique venue in county cricket.

Chapter One
Early cricket in Swansea

Swansea holds a special place in the sporting history of South Wales as the town was the venue during the late 18th century for some of the earliest organised games of cricket on record. Indeed, the first written record of cricket being played in Wales is contained in a letter from a local gentleman to the *General Evening Post* in April 1771 bemoaning the fact that young men gathered together on the Sabbath to take part in a variety of sporting pursuits:

> "football, wrestling, cricket, fighting, jumping and an enormous use of oaths is made their exercise and the pastors of these places generally take too little pains for restraining this vice of profaining the Lord's day."[1]

At the time, there were around 4,500 people living in the town, which had developed into a thriving port at the mouth of the River Tawe, with its success stemming from the shelter provided to the south-west by the Mumbles headland and the absence of sandbanks clogging up the estuary. Swansea was also in the early throws of industrialisation, utilising the easily accessible seams of coal which outcropped close to the surface in the Tawe Valley. In addition to mining activities, the town had become the focus for copper smelting, as entrepreneurs during the first two decades of the 18th century realised that with the process to create one ton of refined copper requiring eighteen tons of coal and thirteen tons of ore it was more economic to bring the ores to the coalfields. By the time the first Census was taken in 1801, Swansea had a population of 6,099 and the seven copper smelters in the Lower Swansea Valley produced around 90% of the total UK output.[2]

In addition to thriving businesses in the Georgian era, the town of Swansea also held pretensions of becoming a fashionable seaside resort. "In point of spirit, fashion and politeness, the Brighton of Wales," was how one regional newspaper described the Copperopolis in August 1786.[3] With wealth from the industrial activities plus the dreams of being the Welsh Weymouth, it was no surprise that Swansea was also the location for one of the first formal cricket clubs in South Wales, as evidenced by a notice in the *Hereford Journal* for May 1785 reminding subscribers to the Swansea club that the first practices of the new season would shortly be taking place, and that members should gather near the Bathing House at Crumlin Burrows. The Bathing House, which was owned by Swansea Corporation, may have been a suitable location for the cricketers to gather, because in addition to changing facilities, there were rooms for dining and dancing. But ten years later the area, like much of the land immediately adjoining

"The Bathing House, Swansea", an engraving by Thomas Rothwell dated 1791 showing the building specially erected for fashionable visitors, as well as the mobile huts which enabled bathing to take place discreetly shielded from public view. West Glamorgan County Hall now stands on the site of the Bathing House.

the Bristol Channel, was inundated by a spring tide and for several years the whole area was a muddy morass.

By the early 19th century, the Burrows had drained sufficiently for a racecourse to be laid out to the east of the river mouth, whilst cricket and other ball games were played on the sands and the meadowland on the western bank. Other folk games such as bando and cock-fighting were held in this area and were so successful that local beer-sellers set up tents on the foreshore from which the thirst of the spectators and participants could be amply quenched.

The Swansea Cricket Club used the wicket on Crumlin Burrows for their practices with the early activities of the Club being akin to a modern-day golf club, with members challenging each other in single- or double-wicket challenges. By 1831 the club had 70 members according to a newspaper article advertising a match between married and single members. The article went on to claim how cricket:

> ".... is likely to become the national game with the Welsh as well as the English and the Swansea Club will yield to few in the number and respectability of its members... Many of the fair sex, attracted by curiosity, or other benevolent motives, were interested spectators of

> the match, and as they could not but observe the scarcity of Benedicts It is to be hoped their compassionate exertions will not be found wanting, in endeavouring to supply the deficiency, by transforming some of the Bachelors into happy members of the opposite party."[4]

Inter-club matches became possible from the 1830s and 1840s as public transport steadily improved and a measure of the standing of Swansea's cricket club can be gauged from the ever-growing members list which now included a number of local dignitaries, including Starling Benson, a leading copper merchant and industrialist, who was elected Mayor of Swansea in 1843. In August of that year he also led the Swansea club in their match at Crumlin Burrows against the Officers of the 73rd and 75th Regiments, with the game having been organised specifically by Capt. Charles Napier, the Chief Constable of Glamorgan, as a goodwill gesture to boost morale in the local area following the unrest caused by the Rebecca Riots.

With the increase in trade, and the arrival of further migrants, there were enough good players in Swansea for the club to field two teams from 1852 onwards. This increase in membership, and the growth of the local economy, also meant that the Swansea club had healthier finances, allowing them to hire decent professionals, whose duties included preparing the wicket as well as coaching. Indeed, the club boasted many junior members, who duly formed their own side, known as the Swansea Juveniles, and also used Crumlin Burrows for their games from the early 1850s.

From 1856 the Burrows were also the venue for the matches staged by Swansea Normal College - their first being in September of that year against Swansea Grammar School, whilst other clubs in the area also played there. The Burrows was also the location of the Swansea racecourse and the report of the match in 1856 against Neath specifically refers to the wicket as being laid out inside the course - whether or not this was common practice remains unclear.

With the town of Swansea growing rapidly, parts of the Burrows were taken over for housing and industry and, as a result, the Club established a Fields Committee during the early 1860s whose task was to seek out alternative locations. In March 1865, they were pleased to report that "The club has succeeded in securing the large field by St Helen's", following agreement with the landowners of Brunswick Court who were happy for the cricket club to use the large field which lay to the south of the house and adjoined the main road running west from the town towards the Oystermouth Road and further west towards the Mumbles. April 1865 saw a trial match at the new ground, known as Brunswick Field, and on 25 May, the first inter-club game on record was held at the new venue as Swansea met the Cadoxton club from Neath.

With the ground close to the burgeoning urban sprawl, the Swansea club were aware that Brunswick Field was unlikely to be their long-term home. With the land prices in the area also rising, the Club's officials were also aware that they could not rely on the kindness of other landowners to provide land at a cheap rent and the question which now occupied the minds of the committee members was how to raise funds to secure a permanent home elsewhere.

The answer was a fund-raising three-day game on 11, 12 and 13 July 1866 between a XXII of Swansea and District against the United All England Eleven - one of the wandering teams of professional players which staged exhibition matches throughout the country. It also saw the Swansea club enter into an agreement with Mr. Pugh, the landlord of the field so that "he agrees to keep the ground clear of all cattle, horses and sheep for the 10th to 14th July so that the committee had free and uncontrolled use."[5] But it was not just about raising money for the Swansea club as the organisation of this match against the crack English professional would have involved appearance fees and other sundry costs such as accommodation. Fortunately, the club had the support of John Talbot Dillwyn Llewelyn, the influential squire of Penllergaer, who was a leading member of the South Wales Cricket Club. The Old Etonian and Oxford-educated industrialist had a wide range of sporting and political contacts in both South Wales and London, and was keen to promote healthy recreation in the Swansea area.

A youthful JTD Llewelyn.

James Livingston.

With Llewelyn acting as a kindly benefactor, it meant that gate money could go straight into the coffers of the Swansea club and the fund they had created for the acquisition of a permanent base. Fortunately, a decent-sized crowd turned up and they were treated to some big hitting by the professionals with one of the English professionals, George Paling, of Nottinghamshire, depositing a series of balls into the back gardens of the houses in Brunswick Street. Besides being a financial success, the timing of the exhibition contest proved to be very good as shortly after the end of the season, the Club were advised by the owners of the Brunswick Field that the land had been earmarked as the site of a new hospital for Swansea.

With the prospect of having to shortly move again, the Club created another

Field Committee. One of its influential members was James Livingston, a distinguished shipbroker in the town and enthusiastic cricketer who also played for Swansea and Glamorgan. He was a man who, in subsequent years took every opportunity to criticise the Swansea Corporation for not setting aside an area in the town for healthy recreation. Indeed, he may have been instrumental for the local newspaper in August 1867 carrying an article in which it was stated:

> "I am surprised by the fact that the [Swansea] corporation - with such means at its disposal - does not make some provision for the healthful recreation of the inhabitants of the town. All available ground is being rapidly built upon. Why not therefore at once secure those (reclaimed) fields on the Mumbles road, by Gorse Lane, for a people's park - a part of which might be reserved as a cricketing ground?"[6]

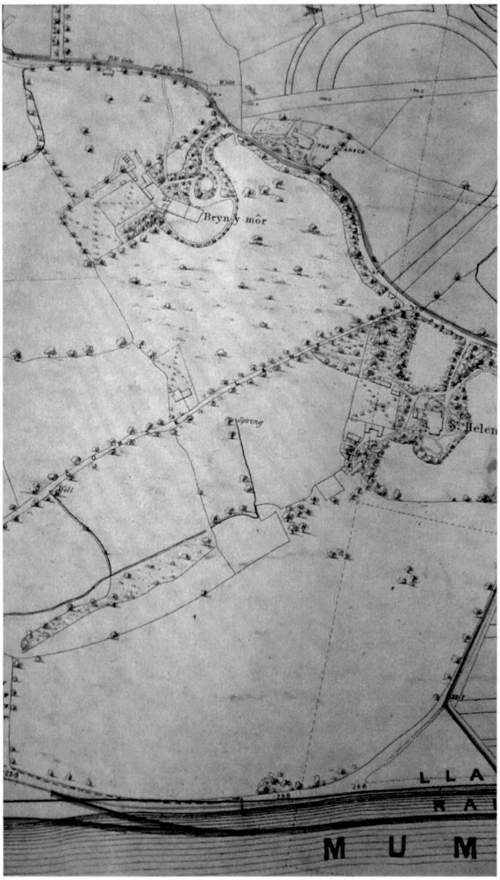

A map of the area to the west of the town of Swansea, dated 1855, showing the Bryn-y-Mor Field.

Livingston was also a leading figure in the negotiations ahead of the 1868 season over a new base with local landowner Robert Eaton, who owned a field, known as Bryn-y-Mor Field on higher ground, a mile or so inland. Together with his good friend JTD Llewelyn, Livingston was delighted with the choice of a new venue and in a bid to raise further funds to enhance the facilities at the Bryn-y-Mor ground, and promote cricket in the area, they made contact with former Surrey cricketer Charles Lawrence who was making negotiations for a tour of the UK later that summer by a team of Aboriginal cricketers. The Swansea officials agreed to the proposal by Lawrence and his business manager, George Smith, a former mayor of Sydney, that the tourists collected all of the gate money, covered all of the expenses and in return gave a £20 donation to the local club.

It duly led to the first-ever visit by an Australian team to Wales with the two-day game in Swansea being one of the 47 matches on the tour, and followed by a third day on which the Aborigines had an opportunity to raise further revenue for themselves with a display of boomerang throwing, spear throwing, sprinting and hurdling. Fittingly, JTD led the home side, taking 6/64, but the tourists proved far too strong for the locals, winning the contest by an innings on the second afternoon, before entertaining a decent-sized crowd the following day with their athletic prowess ahead of travelling by train from the High Street station for their next fixture at Bradford in Yorkshire.

THE AUSTRALIAN BLACK CRICKETERS,
Their only appearance in Wales.

A GRAND CRICKET MATCH will be Played at SWANSEA between ELEVEN of "THE ABORIGINALS" and ELEVEN of the SWANSEA CRICKET CLUB, on MONDAY and TUESDAY, the 6th and 7th July.

On WEDNESDAY, the 8th July, the Blacks will go through their wonderful Feats of THROWING SPEARS and BOOMERANGS, HURDLE and FLAT RACING, &c. See Bills.

Admission to the Field, 1s. each day.

The notice from The Cambrian newspaper promoting the visit of the Australian Aborigines to Swansea in July 1868.

Besides boasting superb views of Swansea Bay, the Bryn-y-Mor Field was adjacent to the Uplands Hotel, a fine local hostelry which quickly developed into a popular meeting point for the town's cricketers. Unlike their previous venues, the cricketers now had a place where they could celebrate a victory, or drown their sorrows after a defeat, as well somewhere for getting changed and holding meetings.[7] The Swansea cricketers certainly enjoyed their summer activities at Bryn-y-Mor and by the early 1870s they decided to maintain their camaraderie by playing football during the winter months. Their first fixture, played against Neath on 23 November, 1872 was played under Association rules, but two years later – perhaps because of the influence of several former public schoolboys - they switched to the rugby union code, and on 14 November 1874 played their inaugural fixture against the young men of Llandovery College.[8]

In their days of just playing cricket at Bryn-y-Mor, the town's eager sportsmen encountered very few occasions when the ground was too wet for matches, but after diversifying into winter games, the pitch frequently became unusable and as one cricketer of the time ruefully commented:

> "the upshot of playing football over the cricket pitch was that the wickets only began to get in decent condition about the end of August."[9]The concerns over the condition of the Bryn-y-Mor wicket were not solely confined to the Swansea area as the MCC dropped their fixture in 1874 with the Swansea Club owing to the poor state of the wicket during the match the previous season. The loss of the prestigious fixture with the MCC was embarrassing for Llewelyn and Livingston but, as you would expect from such influential and astute men of industry and politics, they were already working on a solution.

1. *General Evening Post*, April 1771.
2. J. Alun Owen, *Swansea's Earliest Open Spaces*, Swansea City Council, 1995.
3. *The Gloucester Journal*, 14 August 1786
4. *The Cambrian*, 15 June 1831.
5. Swansea CC minute book, July 6th, 1866.
6. *The Cambrian*, 15 August 1867.
7. Some though enjoyed themselves too much after play at Bryn-y-Mor, with the Swansea CC minute book for April 21st, 1869 noting that "Mr William Bancroft junior had written a letter to apologize for his post-match conduct."
8. *The Cambrian*, 20 November 1874; Brecon County Times, 21 November 1874.
9. *The Cambrian*, 6 September 1878.

Chapter Two
The creation of St. Helen's

With the Copperopolis of Swansea continuing to expand in both economic and geographic terms, it came as no surprise to many that during the early months of 1873 Robert Eaton, the owner of the Bryn-y-Mor Field, agreed to a proposal for house-building on his property. The formal announcement of the proposals was made in The Cambrian newspaper on 21 March, but by this time the cricketers of Swansea were already in discussion with other landowners about an alternative venue. Indeed, the problems with the drainage at Bryn-y-Mor had already led the club to use Primrose Field – a recreation ground in a more central location of the town which subsequently became the headquarters of Swansea's Working Men's Club. It was however, a far from ideal venue for either cricket or rugby as it had a pronounced slope, but at least it was a dry surface.

Indeed, one of the criteria which the re-established Field Committee of the Swansea club had identified as being an important factor in their search for a new venue was drainage. With a plethora of locations with sandy soils on the foreshore of Swansea Bay, JTD Llewelyn and James Livingston made contact during 1872 with Colonel Evan Morgan who leased from Swansea Corporation a strip of land and sand dunes near the St. Helen's tollgate. The scheme which the Swansea officials had hatched involved the

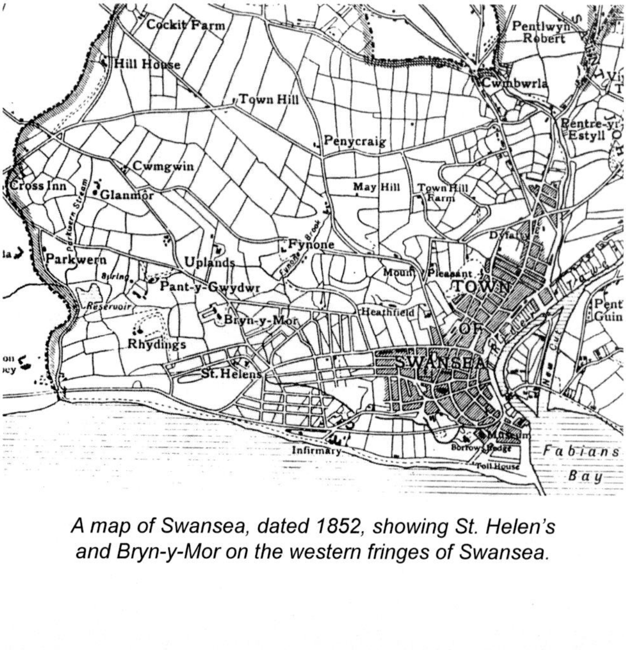

A map of Swansea, dated 1852, showing St. Helen's and Bryn-y-Mor on the western fringes of Swansea.

creation of a freely-drained sports field - suitable for the playing of cricket and rugby - through the further reclamation of sandbanks adjacent to Oystermouth Road.

The negotiations with Colonel Morgan did not go well at first, but by October 1874 and agreement was reached, with local surveyor (and cricketer) Phillip Warren drawing up plans for the new sports field - at a cost of £2,000 - with a level and freely-drained surface. The initial agreement covered a 20 year lease to the cricket club and in the names of JTD and Livingston by Colonel Morgan. The latter however, added a clause that the land would revert to him should building development be permitted by the Corporation. Warren then oversaw the work on creating the new cricket field, with levelling, turfing and rolling of the former sandbanks as well as creating a series of purpose-made wickets. Whilst John Tucker supervised the laying of the turf, the man who was responsible for the creation of the wickets and practice areas was William Bancroft (senior), the patriarch of a sporting family whose name became synonymous with cricket and rugby for many years at the St. Helen's ground.[1]

Born in Barnwell in Cambridgeshire in 1824, William (senior) took up a boot-making apprenticeship in his early teens in Cambridge, before getting married and moving to Bury St. Edmunds in Suffolk. During the early 1850s, he moved again, with his wife and young child, to Shoreditch in London, with their move to the capital being not entirely related to William's desire to develop his boot-making skills. Instead, it was cricketing reasons as he also had shown great promise as a cricketer whilst in Cambridgeshire and Suffolk, and held ambitions to become a professional cricketer, believing that he might gain a trial as a professional bowler with the MCC.

Whilst there are no surviving records of him having a trial at Lord's, legions of Welsh sportsmen have become eternally grateful that he moved to London as during his time in the city, he became aware of a professional appointment with the ambitious Swansea club. It is not known whether he was spotted by an official from the Welsh club, or whether he was personally recommended by someone who had seen him perform in the London area, but the 1861 Census dutifully records the expanding Bancroft family as being residents of Swansea, with William plying his trade as a bootmaker, and playing as a professional for the town's cricket club.

His move to Swansea was hugely successful as he quickly became one of the leading professionals in South Wales, with the all-rounder being regularly chosen for the Glamorganshire side which played a number of inter-county fixtures during the 1860s, including their inaugural fixture against Carmarthenshire at Llanelli in August 1861. Bancroft batted regularly in the top-order, and proved to be a consistent run-scorer in these days of round-arm and under arm bowling. On several occasions, he also showed his own prowess with the ball, including a fine return of 6/64 in the match against Carmarthenshire at Neath in 1864.

His duties with the Swansea club also included coaching and helping

William Bancroft (senior).

to groom the next generation of sportsmen. By the late 1860s, he was regarded as one of the finest coaches in the region, as evidenced by his selection as captain of the Colts XXII in 1869 which played the newly formed Glamorganshire side in a two-day encounter at Neath. His skills as a groundsman were also highly regarded and having helped to create a decent surface at Bryn-y-Mor, the acquisition of the land adjacent to the Oystermouth Road gave him a fresh challenge and during the early 1870s he played a key role in the laying of turf on the reclaimed sand dunes besides overseeing the creation of a series of pitches, with Llewelyn also dipping into his pocket to create a wall around the new ground. Perhaps as a thank you, Llewelyn also ensured that the plans for the new ground included the creation of a cottage built adjacent on the Oystermouth Road, and a home from which William and his growing family could tend not just the cricket field, but also the rugby pitch alongside, besides coaching the members of the Club in the area of practice nets which had also been created adjacent to Gorse Lane.

1874 duly saw the final matches of cricket and rugby at the Bryn-y-Mor Field and, with developments at St. Helen's having taking place smoothly, the grand opening of the new ground occurred on Whit Monday 1875 with an estimated 7,000 people present for a series of athletics events organised by the cricket club. With cricket still being the major sport, the new sports field was frequently referred to, during the course of the next few years, as 'The New Cricket Field, St. Helen's.' However, the rugby section was not forgotten, with Llewelyn continuing to give his support to the club, by helping to finance the building of a new and more spacious pavilion in 1878 to replace the smaller and basic one initially constructed with a decent sized dressing room adjacent to Bryn Road to serve both the summer and winter games. The new ground swiftly became popular and within a couple of years a second wicket was created, on the rugby ground itself, for the use of the junior clubs in the area.

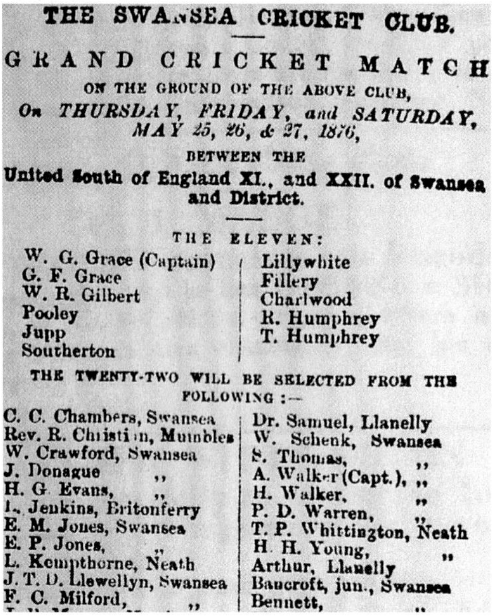

THE SWANSEA CRICKET CLUB.

GRAND CRICKET MATCH

ON THE GROUND OF THE ABOVE CLUB,

On THURSDAY, FRIDAY, and SATURDAY, MAY 25, 26, & 27, 1876,

BETWEEN THE

United South of England XI., and XXII. of Swansea and District.

THE ELEVEN:

W. G. Grace (Captain)	Lillywhite
G. F. Grace	Fillery
W. R. Gilbert	Charlwood
Pooley	R. Humphrey
Jupp	T. Humphrey
Southerton	

THE TWENTY-TWO WILL BE SELECTED FROM THE FOLLOWING :—

C. C. Chambers, Swansea	Dr. Samuel, Llanelly
Rev. R. Christian, Mumbles	W. Schenk, Swansea
W. Crawford, Swansea	S. Thomas, "
J. Donague "	A. Walker (Capt.), "
H. G. Evans, "	H. Walker, "
L. Jenkins, Britonferry	P. D. Warren, "
E. M. Jones, Swansea	T. P. Whittington, Neath
E. P. Jones, "	H. H. Young, "
L. Kempthorne, Neath	Arthur, Llanelly
J. T. D. Llewellyn, Swansea	Bancroft, jun., Swansea
F. C. Milford, "	Bennett, "

A newspaper advert promoting the visit of the United South of England team in 1876.

Through the efforts of Bancroft and the patronage of Llewelyn and Livingston, plus the support of other traders and businessmen in Swansea, the St. Helen's ground became the best equipped venue in the area and one which could rival Cardiff's facilities at the Arms Park. An indication of this came with the arrangements for a three-day game between a XXII of Swansea and District against a United South of England XI in May 1876, The United XI included WG Grace and the good doctor really enjoyed himself as he made 51 in the England team's first innings before claiming fifteen wickets when the Swansea team batted, including both JTD Llewelyn and William Bancroft

The locals were dismissed for 40, leaving the United side with a target of 75, but John Parnham, the left-arm spinner who was the professional at Llandovery College, claimed five wickets, including those of both WG and Fred Grace, to set up a tense finish. The situation seemed however to be too much for the scorers, as the local newspaper reported:

> "the finish of the game was extremely exciting with the last man sent to the wicket, Dr. Bramhall [a late replacement for one of the professionals] having only one run to make to win the game. But when he was cleverly bowled by Platts, amidst the enthusiastic shouts of the Twenty-Two and the ringing applause of the spectators, the match thus ended in a tie. There was however some dispute respecting the score, but we understand that it was agreed that it should stand as a tie."[2]

Two years later, St. Helen's staged a two-day game between the South Wales Club and the Australian tourists. Securing the game was a major coup for Llewelyn, who that year was High Sheriff of Glamorgan and his friends as it was the first time that a major match had been staged between the Welsh regional side and an international touring team. As a Director of the Great Western Railway, he also used his many contacts with the local railway companies to organise the running of additional trains with reduced fares to Swansea, whilst many shop owners agreed to half-day closing so that as many people as possible could get to St. Helen's and see in the flesh the tourists who the winter before had taken part in the inaugural Test Match.[3]

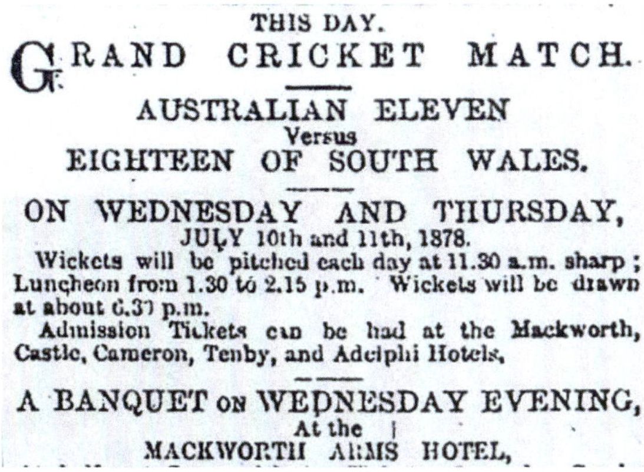
THIS DAY.

GRAND CRICKET MATCH.

AUSTRALIAN ELEVEN
Versus
EIGHTEEN OF SOUTH WALES.

ON WEDNESDAY AND THURSDAY,
JULY 10th and 11th, 1878.

Wickets will be pitched each day at 11.30 a.m. sharp; Luncheon from 1.30 to 2.15 p.m. Wickets will be drawn at about 6.30 p.m.

Admission Tickets can be had at the Mackworth, Castle, Cameron, Tenby, and Adelphi Hotels.

A BANQUET ON WEDNESDAY EVENING,
At the
MACKWORTH ARMS HOTEL,

A newspaper notice promoting the match at Swansea against the 1878 Australians.

Originally it was agreed that the tourists would travel to Swansea to play an eleven-a-side match on 8th and 9th July but after arriving in England, the tourists agreed to play another fixture at Twickenham on those days. The fixture at Swansea was therefore put back a couple of days, and after their outstanding form shown in the early part of their tour, the conditions of the match were further amended so that the South Wales side, assembled and captained by Llewelyn, could field eighteen players against the men from the Antipodes.

The tourists included Fred Spofforth, nicknamed 'The Demon', as the first man to exploit modern-style overarm bowling to its fullest extent. The bounce and movement he extracted made him too much for even the best batsmen in the UK, let alone the club-standard players he bowled against on much of the tour. "This Spofforth throws his arms about like a windmill," said one local observer." He deceived the batsmen by delivering many moderate balls with all the appearance of a very fast one."[4]

They were also a hairy crowd, the 1878 Australians, at a time when full beards and elaborate moustaches were fashionable. Indeed, they looked more like bushrangers than cricketers, none more so than their captain

Dave Gregory, later famous - or notorious - for telling the mighty Lord Harris where he got off. But the tourists were a pretty tired bunch, having got in at 4.30 a.m. after a nightmare journey from Twickenham, John Moore of Neath, the Secretary of the South Wales CC, under whose aegis the fixture had been arranged, had been fretting all week that the Australians would not bother to make the 200 mile journey to meet an obscure Welsh side, but they honoured the fixture with the two umpires - Willaim Bancroft (senior) and James Lillywhite junior - walking out to the middle as play began on time at 11.30 a.m. after JTD won the toss and following a chat with his team, invited the Australians to bat first, hoping that they were still weary after their long, overnight journey.

JTD also delivered the first over with the Bannerman brothers, Charles and Alec, at the crease. He had an easy action, bowling off-cutters, but his first ball was short of a length and Charles Bannerman leant back and elegantly cut it for four. Sharing the new ball was Charles Prytherch Lewis, a fine all-round sportsman, educated at Llandovery College and Oxford University and a man who a few years later was in the first wave of Welsh rugby internationals. He was a much quicker bowler than JTD with a low slinging delivery. His first ball slammed into Alec Bannerman's thin gloves, jarring his fingers before shortly afterwards getting a delivery to rear up at Charles Bannerman with the ball flying off the edge of his bat and through the hands of the fielder of short-leg for three runs. Another short ball followed in his next over - this time Alec Bannerman missed it, but Edgar Davies, who was keeping wicket for the South Wales team did not. However, in taking the ball, the solicitor from Crickhowell split the webbing on his hand and with blood seeping out from his gauntlets, he left the field for treatment leaving his side without a regular gloveman for the rest of the game.

After half an hour or so, Thomas Babington Jones replaced JTD with the Oxford Blue from Brecon delivering his brisk off-breaks. His first over was a maiden, before Charles Bannerman took a liking to Jones' bowling, with a couple of drives and cuts bringing the Australian further boundaries. Lewis continued at the other end and his mood was not improved as another edge was dropped at slip. But it did not prove to be too expensive a miss as two balls later, a ball breached Bannerman's defensive stroke and knocked back off and middle stumps.

With the tourists on 37-1, Tom Horan made his way to the middle, sporting enormous bushy sideburns and wearing a curiously shaped white hat with a broad peak all the way around. His arrival saw the introduction into the attack of Frank Cobden, the famous Cambridge University bowler who had settled in Mid Wales. He was not the Cobden of eight years before, when he had prevented Oxford winning the Varsity match by taking the last three wickets in as many balls. In his prime, at 12 stone, he had been a fast bowler. Now with a larger waistline he had lost some pace but, even so, he was still able to find the edge of Alec Bannerman's bat as he tried to cut a ball too close to him, got a top edge and was caught at third man.

Cobden claimed a second wickets as Dave Gregory, pushed forward with

Frank Cobden.

TB Jones.

bat and beard, and popped up a ball straight into JTD's hands at short leg, but the two Toms - Horan and Garrett - threatened to cut loose and it was only the smart fielding of Cardiff's Cuthbert Riches in the covers which prevented a series of boundaries. But just as it seemed Horan might cut loose during the afternoon, he departed in the over before lunch as a ricochet off his thigh saw the ball cannon into the stumps. The runs continued to flow during the afternoon as Billy Murdoch, George Bailey and Jack Conway all unleashed some furious blows, but Cobden and Lewis stuck to their task, with the latter running through the lower order, though not before Harry Boyle had a further chance to expose the sloppiness of the Welsh fielding by running five for a stroke to fine-leg.

With the Australians having made 219, Riches and Bertie Young, an engineer with the Vale of Neath Railway, began the Welsh side's reply with Spofforth and Boyle commencing the bowling. Riches blocked all four balls of Spofforth's first over, but in the Australian's next over he spliced a rising ball from the paceman into the hands of point. Young then edged Boyle to slip before Gerry Elkington, a stylish off-side player from Carmarthenshire became Spofforth's second victim as he was caught behind. Next ball, the fast bowler sent Cobden's middle stump flying out of the ground before Edward Curteis, an Army captain from Brecon, drew on all of his military resolve as he blocked the hat trick ball.

It wasn't long though before Spofforth made further inroads into the valiant Welsh batting before Lewis came in and used the long handle with some effect for three quarters of hour. The Oxford Blue struck a brace of aerial blows, each just out of the grasping hands of the fielders and after one near catch, Spofforth gave him one of the Mephistophelian looks which provoked his nickname. Shortly afterwards, the enraged bowler delivered a ball which sent two of Lewis' stumps cartwheeling out of the ground with one nearly hitting wicketkeeper Jack Blackham in the face. A few overs later he showed little respect as JTD walked out to bat. The squire of Penllergaer was greeted by a fast short ball that arrived chest high. JTD pushed a tentative bat at it and Charles Bannerman took another catch at point. A few minutes later the innings came to an end as the South Wales gentlemen were dismissed for 94 with Spofforth finishing with 10/35.

They followed on the following morning at 11.30 with the crowd of 3,000 hoping for a spirited fightback. It was not to be as by 3.30 p.m. they were all out again for 88. Second time around, it was the steady seam of Boyle that caused the damage, with the Australian taking 9/33 as they hurried to an innings victory and allowed them an early getaway for their next fixture in Lancashire. At the evening banquet JTD philosophised on why the colonial side had proved too strong - not just for South Wales, but for the best players in England. "Perhaps it is because a country like Australia, where men have to work hard in every trade, where perhaps the luxuries of life are not so well marked as in Britain, will naturally produce finer men," he said.

The game had admittedly been something of a mismatch, and showed JTD and the other enthusiastic officials who attended from across South Wales that a lot of hard work remained to be done before the cricketers of the region could mount a challenge against the visiting Test players, never mind challenge them on equal terms. There was plenty of optimism though to be taken about the new facilities at St. Helen's and the first purpose-built cricket ground in the region. The Australians had been complimentary about the new ground and whilst the standard of play in

The Swansea RFC team of 1879/80 in front of the new pavillion paid for by JTD Llewelyn (image reproduced courtesy of the City and Council of Swansea, Swansea Museum Collection).

the home side left something to be desired, the cricketers of the region now had first-class facilities at the new Swansea ground. As JTD mentioned during a speech at a grand Banquet at the Mackworth Arms, "things are certainly on the up for the cricketers of South Wales."[5]

But there was another agenda behind the visit of the 1878 Australians to St. Helen's, as an increasingly vocal lobby existed within Swansea Corporation in the vicinity of the cricket field, including the field on the eastern side of Gorse Lane, now known as Victoria Park. A riposte came from the Mayor of Swansea during the function at the Mackworth Arms, with the civic leader stating that:

> "he would move heaven and earth to prevent Colonel Morgan's field being built over. It was clearly the duty of towns to provide open spaces for recreational purposes so that the rising generation may grow to be healthy, happy and well-developed."[6]

The St. Helen's ground, seen in 1903.

In contrast, The "Build on St. Helen's" lobby argued that the executors of the late Colonel Morgan were prepared to surrender their leasehold interest for the sum of £10,000 and with arguments for and against being played out in the columns of local newspapers, the Mayor convened a public meeting. JTD nailed his colours to the mast by saying beforehand that:

> "saving St. Helen's from the encroachment of unromantic lines of bricks and mortar which puts flight all rural sweets and compels the weary denizen of the town to seek them from afar"[7]

He also addressed the public meeting and argued passionately in favour of the recreational facilities as well as deploring the absence of the

Mayor himself, who did not appear at the meeting. JTD had a great ally in Alderman William Thomas of Lan, a man known locally as "the pioneer of open spaces". He had previously worked with JTD over what became known as Parc Llewelyn, and for the public meeting over the future of the land to the east of Gorse Lane, known as St. Helen's Field, he assembled a compendium of testimonials plus a document signed by 800 people who supported the use of the area for healthy recreation. The Corporation deferred a decision about the future of St. Helen's, as the dispute rumbled on for several years. But these were finally defeated in December 1885 when Alderman Thomas won a vote in favour of the St. Helen's Field being used for recreational purposes and *The Cambrian* newspaper proclaiming:

> "Alderman Thomas is to be congratulated ...having fought the prolonged fight and fairly won the battle in retaining the St. Helen's Field as an open space for the use of the public."[8]

An aerial view of St. Helen's and Victoria Park taken during the late 1920s showing the foreshore of Swansea Bay.

1. *The Cambrian*, 16 October, 23 October and 6 November 1874. PD Warren was born in London in 1851 and left Swansea in 1878 to work in Ceylon. He became Surveyor-General of Ceylon in 1904.
2. *South Wales Daily News*, 29 May 1876.
3. *South Wales Daily News*, 10 July 1878.
4. *South Wales Daily News*, 11 July 1878.
5. *The Cambrian*, 12 July 1878.
6. ibid
7. *The Cambrian*, 21 March 1879.
8. *The Cambrian*, 24 December 1885.

Chapter Three
The Bancrofts

It was not just William Bancroft (senior) who played a leading role in establishing St. Helen's as a fine sporting venue. His son William (junior) and grandson Billy went on to be major influences in both the summer and winter recreational activities at the Swansea ground. It was perhaps inevitable given the relationship between JTD and the Bancrofts that William Bancroft (junior) should continue the good name of the family in cricketing circles in South Wales, as well as further afield from his home in Swansea. His formative years were spent at the Bryn-y-Mor ground, playing for the Swansea Colts, and the town's 1st XI, in addition to being coached by his doting father who took much pleasure in passing on tips to his enthusiastic son.

Indeed, at the age of sixteen - William (junior) was chosen to play for the Glamorganshire side against Carmarthenshire at The Gnoll in Neath in 1864. Any nerves that he may have had were quelled as his father was also in the Glamorgan side, along with several of his friends from the Swansea club, including JTD who had helped to assemble the side. A measure of the high regard JTD had for the schoolboy can be gauged from the fact that young Bancroft opened the batting with the Squire of Penllergaer - a man who was to play a major role in his adult life.

The summer of 1868 was the first milestone in Bancroft's playing career as that summer he recorded his inaugural half-century at county level, making 51 against Breconshire, besides appearing in the match at Bryn-y-Mor against the Australian Aborigines. He also showed prowess with the ball, taking eleven wickets in the county's match in 1869 against Radnorshire. A bright future was therefore forecast for young Bancroft, but with his father still employed by the Swansea club, there were not any immediate openings in the Swansea area.

Having completed his apprenticeship as a boot-maker, William (junior) could have focussed instead on this, but cricket was his love, and like his father before him, he realised that he could broaden his experience by moving away from the family home. With offers coming in from clubs over the border, the all-rounder decided to further his career by playing as a professional with Settle, Dunfermline, and Merchiston Castle. Despite these engagements in Northern England and Scotland, Bancroft regularly accepted invitations from JTD to play for the South Wales CC on their annual visits to London and the south-east.

Despite having to make some long and tiring journeys by train, young Bancroft no doubt hoped that some decent performances at Lord's and The Oval would help him secure lucrative offers from other clubs. But

William Bancroft (junior).

following the creation of the St. Helen's ground, it was only a matter of time before his return to Swansea soil and, having served his apprenticeship elsewhere, he duly succeeded his father as the Swansea professional.

Once again, JTD played a role in securing his services, with Bancroft's income from his work at St. Helen's being augmented by coaching pupils at Swansea Grammar School, in addition to acting as private coach to the Llewelyn family at Penllergaer and working alongside 'Sam' Lovering in tending the wicket for the Cadoxton club. As a result, Bancroft was able to earn a lucrative earning as a professional cricketer, supplemented by working alongside his father in tending the Swansea ground as well as repairing the footwear of local sportsmen.

At the time, William (junior) was the finest home-grown all-rounder in South Wales, and it was a shame that the winding-up of the Glamorganshire club in 1874 prevented him from regularly playing at county level when he was at his peak with bat and ball. In 1885 he gave a glimpse of what might have been by scoring a fine half-century for the South Wales CC against Worcestershire, whilst later in the season he scored an outstanding 97 against the MCC. By the time Glamorgan CCC had been created, Bancroft's skills as a batsman were on the wane, but the good name of the family was maintained by his young son Billy, whilst JTD's sons Willie and Charlie each won selection in the county side and showed that they had benefited greatly from his tutelage.

Willie Llewelyn.

Charlie Llewelyn.

Tragically, Willie committed suicide in the grounds of his family's home at Penllergaer in 1891 with his loss being deeply felt by both father and tutor alike. He had been due to play the following day for Glamorgan against Devon at Swansea, and with several amateurs unable to play at such short notice, it was William (junior) who came into the county side and was set to play alongside Billy.

The veteran professional never got onto the field as rain washed out play after just a handful of over in Glamorgan's 1st innings. But the following year, the two Bancrofts managed to take the field together for Glamorgan at Swansea - and in much happier circumstances - as the county played a Colts team, several of whom had also benefited from William's wise words in the nets at the Swansea ground.

To the delight of his father and grandfather, Billy Bancroft upheld the fine name of the family by becoming Glamorgan`s first-ever full-time professional player in 1895. His appointment however, came at a most interesting time in the life of the 24-year old sportsman who was playing county cricket and international rugby. Growing up at the St. Helen's ground, it was no surprise that Billy inherited his father's and grandfather's love of cricket, besides acquiring a desire for rugby and developing his ball skills in the winter game, but it meant that he became a paid player in the summer and an amateur, in theory, in the winter.

Billy's first appearance for Glamorgan had been in 1889 as he played in Glamorgan's inaugural county match against Warwickshire at the Arms Park, before making his debut for Swansea's 1st XV in October. So impressive was the strong and confident-running full-back that the following February he was drafted into the Welsh side, with the Swansea-born man winning the first of 33 Welsh caps. His prowess at rugby was no surprise given the fact that from boyhood he spent around two hours per day kicking, running and catching the ball on his family's hallowed turf at St. Helen's. These were invaluable skills given his slight frame, and

The Bancrofts in front of their cottage on the St. Helen's ground where the family lived until it was demolished in 1891.

his kicking on the run was a highly prized skill, learnt after many years of practice on the outfield adjacent to his family's cottage.

However, Wales only won two out of Bancroft's first nine appearances and a few questions were raised about his defensive capabilities. These were swiftly answered in 1893 as Wales, under the captaincy of Arthur Gould, won the Triple Crown for the first-ever time. The first match of that season saw England visit the Arms Park - a venue where Wales had never previously defeated England - and in the days leading up to the game, there were doubts that the game would go-ahead, before eighteen tons of coal were burned in braziers on the night before the game to prevent the frost getting at the pitch.

It did the trick, and a thrilling game ensued, with England leading Wales 11-9 until a couple of minutes before the final whistle when Wales were awarded a penalty kick, about thirty yards out and just in from the touch-line. Gould called up Bancroft, who insisted on drop kicking the ball rather than opting to place kick. Gould initially disagreed, but Bancroft convinced him that he could win the game. After a heated exchange, Bancroft duly slotted the ball over the posts, and after subsequent victories over Scotland and Ireland, Wales lifted the Triple Crown.

Bancroft returned to Swansea as a hero, but despite many fine words on his behalf, plus some magnanimous gestures, he did not derive any financial benefit from Wales' success as rugby was still an amateur sport. In fact, at the time, cricket was Billy's main source of income, based on his professional duties with Swansea, topped up by appearances for Glamorgan, and supplemented by his earnings, working alongside his father repairing boots and shoes.

Billy Bancroft – in his winter and summer kit.

1894 saw Billy enjoy his most successful season to date with the bat for Glamorgan. Previously he had recorded solitary fifties in 1891, 1892 and 1893, but in 1894 alone Bancroft scored no less than four fifties, against the MCC and Monmouthshire. By the end of the summer, his stock as an all-round sportsman was in the ascent, and a lucrative offer came his way from Wiltshire to join them as a professional for the 1895 season.

For a couple of weeks, it looked as if Glamorgan's most promising young player would accept the offer which, at the end of the day, would more than provide him with financial security. The reaction however from sporting circles in Swansea was one of complete shock, and public meetings were held in the town to discuss the issues. A couple of other, highly successful Swansea rugby players had previously turned professional by going 'north', and playing rugby league for teams based in Lancashire and Yorkshire, and for a while, it looked as if Billy Bancroft would also leave South Wales.

Not for the first time, JTD solved a potentially tricky situation by suggesting to Jack Brain, the Glamorgan captain, that the Welsh county themselves should offer Billy decent terms to be a full-time professional. This was in keeping with Jack's thoughts, especially his musing over how the county could become a more professional outfit. On several occasions, amateurs had failed to turn up for matches, and hiring more professional players on a decent retainer was one option, although one with a price for the Welsh county.

However, the committee saw the logic in having a regular professional, especially someone who was locally born and, like Billy, was well-known to the sporting public. However, the sticking point was the quite modest sum that the committee originally had in mind, and it may have been no coincidence that around this time, news filtered through about the more lucrative offer to Billy from Wiltshire.

Soon after hearing about the details from the Chippenham club, JTD made some more diplomatic noises, as well as dipping into his pocket, allowing more generous terms to be offered. To the delight of sporting fans in Swansea, Billy quickly agreed terms with Glamorgan, allowing him to remain with Swansea RFC. His fee with Glamorgan was the princely amount of £2 per week for twenty weeks, allowing him to continue in the rather paradoxical situation of representing Glamorgan as a professional sportsman during the summer, whilst in the winter, playing as an amateur rugby player for Wales.

His career subsequently blossomed, with Billy subsequently leading Wales on eleven occasions from 1898, including their Triple Crown win in 1900. He also developed a reputation of being one of the game's finest kickers – a richly deserved honour at a time when games were staged using heavy, leather balls. Despite often being saturated with water and mud, Billy developed a skill to almost nonchalantly drop or place kick a ball with unerring accuracy. Another party piece saw him catch the ball, before waiting for the opposition to run towards him, but just before they were poised to tackle him, he would jink and quickly dart away, leaving the would-be tackler sprawling on the floor.

As far as Billy's cricketing career was concerned, he recorded his maiden county century in 1896, with an unbeaten 119 against Monmouthshire, and for the next dozen years he was a stalwart presence in the Glamorgan middle-order side as, from 1897, they played in the Minor County Championship. In 1899 he enjoyed a fine game against Surrey 2nd XI, scoring 102, and taking a career-best 5/20 with his seam bowling. However, his finest match in Glamorgan ranks came in 1903, fittingly on his home ground in Swansea, as he made 207.

The local newspapers were full of praise for his efforts with the *Evening Express* saying "his finely played innings re-established his reputation, for he gave fewer chances than usual to the fielders."[1]. Berkshire were on the receiving end again in 1905, as he made his fourth hundred for Glamorgan with a solid 105, and during the course of the next four years, Billy added centuries to his tally against Northumberland, Devon and Cornwall.

20 June 1912 was a standout date both for Billy and the St. Helen's ground as the all-rounder appeared for South Wales in the inaugural first-class fixture staged at Swansea. A combined Glamorgan and Monmouthshire side had played the touring teams since 1905, but the three-day match against the 1912 South Africans was the only one to be staged at St. Helen's, and the only one to be awarded first-class status. It came at a time when Glamorgan's campaign for elevation into the County Championship was gaining support, and the need for another lucrative venue, in addition to the Arms Park for marquee games, was uppermost in the administrators thinking.

1912 saw a triangular series with both Australia and South Africa playing in a series against England, and with a match against the Australians scheduled for August at the Arms Park, the opportunity of staging a match against the Springboks at St. Helen's presented an ideal opportunity for the Swansea club to showcase their facilities for a major cricket match.

The decision met with great excitement in the Swansea area, with additional seating being hired to line the rugby field boundary and, also at the Mumbles Road End. The lofty grandstand, built in 1891/92, also provided decent seating. With increased expenditure, plus a guarantee to be paid to the Springboks, the Swansea authorities agreed to the suggestion by the Glamorgan committee to raise admission from sixpence to a shilling. With plenty of rain in the days leading up to contest, there was concern about how events would unfold, as outlined in a report in the *Western Mail*:

> "Swansea has been on tenterhooks for the past few days owing to the uncertainty of the weather. The reputation of the town in the matter of getting a profitable crowd is now at stake."[2]

The tourists arrived the night before by train from Bath in overcast and drizzly conditions, and there was still a bit of dampness around as they, and the South Wales team, gently limbered up ahead of the toss. With uncertainty about the start time, only 500 people were present when Louis Tancred and Herbie Taylor walked out to bat after the tourists had elected to bat, but this increased nearly ten fold by mid-afternoon as the locals watched the Springboks ease to 352, with Sid Pegler adding some lusty blows late in the innings as he struck spinner and assistant groundsman Harry Creber for a brace of sixes into the Mumbles Road.

Billy held a catch at mid-off to remove Claude Carter, before opening the batting with Norman Riches as the South Wales side began their reply with 35 minutes play remaining. But Billy's stay at the wicket proved to be a brief one as after a couple of drives he was bowled by Dave Nourse. The left-arm seamer made further inroads the following morning and with Pegler's leg-breaks filleting the middle-order, the Welsh side were in danger of following-on and potentially losing inside two days.

Noel Phillips of Monmouthshire, plus the Glamorgan pairing of Henry Symonds and Tom Whittington offered some stout resistance before the Welsh side were dismissed for 192. To the relief of the Glamorgan and Swansea officials, Frank Mitchell opted to bat again rather than enforce the follow-on – "a grand sporting gesture" proclaimed the *South Wales Evening Post* whose correspondent was very well aware of the sizeable loss an early finish would create.[3]

Stan Hacker, the former Gloucestershire fast bowler who was now delivering brisk cutters, took the honours when the tourists batted again with Mitchell himself top-scoring against a Welsh attack that was missing Harry Creber who had a shoulder strain, and no doubt some bruised pride, after the onslaught by the Yorkshire-born batsman first time around. When the last Springbok wicket fell, the South Wales side were left with a target of 365, or more realistically three and three-quarter hours in which to hold on for a morale-boosting draw.

In the second innings, Billy opened the batting with Arthur Webb, the former Hampshire batsman, as Norman Riches was having a massage having also jarred his shoulder whilst keeping wicket. In his absence, Billy and Arthur began well against the seamers, but on 16 Billy was bowled by Aubrey Faulkner. The canny purveyor of leg-breaks and googlies then exploited the wearing wicket, claiming 7/67 as the home side were dismissed inside 53 overs to give the South Africans a handsome victory by 230 runs prior to their long journey by the London and North Western Railway's evening express to Glasgow for their match at Hamilton Crescent against Scotland. They were not the only ones to leave St. Helen's with a smile on their face, as later that evening, the Glamorgan officials, having totted up all the cash taken at the gates, announced that takings of £230 on the final day had meant that the guarantee and expenses had been covered, and that a small profit had been generated.[4]

Although there was delight amongst the Swansea ranks over the financial arrangements of the game, the sizeable defeat had shown that there was still much work to be done on the playing side before Glamorgan could realistically press for first-class status. In the meantime, the Swansea contingent on the Glamorgan committee looked at other ways of capitalising on the interest which the South African match had aroused. With no touring team scheduled for 1913, they successfully lobbied for back-to-back matches in mid-August at St. Helen's as an experiment was undertaken to stage a Cricket Week at Swansea

The Glamorgan officials were fully aware of the success of similar festivals staged by Gloucestershire at Cheltenham College, and by Yorkshire at Scarborough, and with the Mumbles burgeoning reputation as a genteel Edwardian resort, plus the excellent communications from Swansea afforded by the Mumbles Railway, the Club's officials looked to tap into the tourist trade. To their delight, the matches against Kent 2nd XI and Wiltshire again drew decent crowds, so for 1914 the Glamorgan committee decided to split the six-match allocation of home matches equally between Cardiff and Swansea, with the St. Helen's ground staging their quota back-to-back from 6 July to 11 July.

It also spoke volumes about the abilities of Creber and the Bancroft family in preparing suitable wickets and net facilities for six successive days of county cricket. The festival of county cricket at Swansea in 1914 began with a two-day friendly which had been arranged with Northamptonshire, the most recent side to be elevated from the Minor County ranks into the County Championship.

With Glamorgan's campaign to follow suit gaining momentum, the contest with the East Midlands side gave the Welsh county another chance of showcasing the rising talent, as well as assessing the attributes of several professionals with first-class experience who were performing well in the local leagues and were looking to qualify for Glamorgan. As far as Eddie

Bates, the former Yorkshire batsman, was concerned, it was a successful audition, as the Yorkshireman who was now playing for Briton Ferry Town and who would go on to play for Glamorgan until 1931, made a composed half-century.

With the selectors having an eye to the future, Billy did not appear in the match with Northamptonshire, nor was he chosen in the squad for the Minor County Championship matches which followed against Durham and Essex 2nd XI with the Glamorgan authorities giving an opportunity to Bill Bestwick, the former Derbyshire fast bowler, who was enjoying a successful season with Neath and had verbally agreed with Glamorgan officials to qualify for the Club. It was though something of a gamble for them, giving Bestwick's chequered past with Derbyshire.

The former miner had first played for Derbyshire in 1898 and over the next decade became the bulwark of their attack. But he also developed a reputation for heavy drinking and in 1906 was also accused of killing a man after a bar-room scuffle. Charges of unlawful killing were later dropped, as the inquest jury ruled that he had acted in self-defence as the other man repeatedly lunged at him with a knife. But the accusations tarnished his reputation and after a series of heavy drinking bouts, he was released by Derbyshire in 1909.[5]

Bill was clearly a troubled man and in need of a fresh start in another area. After a spell in the Lancashire League, he moved to South Wales during 1912, where he initially played and worked in Merthyr Tydfil before joining the Neath club. It proved in many ways to be a good move, as he met and married his second wife, who became something of a calming influence on him as he began what he hoped would be a second chance in county cricket with Glamorgan.

He duly marked his debut for the Welsh county with a haul of 6/44 in Durham's first innings, with the correspondent of the *South Wales Evening Post* commenting how Bill "with his strong arms and burly shoulders extracted pace and lift from what had appeared to be a fairly docile surface."[6] Indeed, after Durham had been dismissed for 137, the wicket, and Bill's bowling performance was put into context as Norman Riches and Jock Tait shared an opening partnership of 103.

But the glee shown by the Glamorgan hierarchy in having seemingly unearthed a bowling gem soon evaporated as the officials from Neath CC belatedly confirmed that they would require Bestwick's services for their League match on the following Saturday - the second day of the match against Essex 2nd XI. News that Bestwick was unavailable only came on the Friday morning as the players were practicing ahead of the final game of the Festival week.

As with the other matches that week, Billy Bancroft lent a hand bowling in the nets having helped Creber and others put the finishing touches to the wicket. The 43 year-old had played for the county side in early June in their away matches at The Oval and Sunderland, so he was hastily drafted into the side by Norman Riches. At first, it did not look like being a great decision as he was bowled first ball by Harry Smith, but Billy responded with typical grit in the second innings as he made an unbeaten 81, batting for two and a quarter hours, striking a six and seven fours as together with team-mate James Maxwell the pair helped Glamorgan set Essex a target of 336 on the final afternoon.[7]

The game against Essex 2nd XI ended in a draw, and proved to be Billy Bancroft's final appearance for Glamorgan on his home soil. In later years, the old stager was mightily pleased about his final innings for the Welsh county and was present at St. Helen's as Bill Bestwick continued his roller-coaster career in professional cricket. Having played again for Glamorgan in 1920 the former miner looked set to play for the Welsh county as first-class status was finally secured for 1921.

But his native county stepped in with a better offer and it was for Derbyshire that Bestwick appeared during the 1920s including the game with Glamorgan at Swansea in 1922. Just to rub salt into the wounds, he claimed eight wickets in the Peakites victory at St. Helen's by 283 runs, having the previous year taken all ten in Glamorgan's second innings at the Arms Park.

On both occasions, his return to Welsh soil saw a group of his old friends from The Gnoll meet up with the burly bowler after play for a few beers. At the Arms Park, his friends had travelled to Cardiff, but in 1922 Bill headed after play to Neath with his pals decision not to go into Swansea, like the late decision over Bill's availability for the Essex match in 1914, highlighting the long-standing tensions between the two towns and their sportsmen, as well as the other local rivalries which had long been part of sport in south-west Wales.

1. *Evening Express*, 9 July 1903.
2. *Western Mail*, 20 June 1912.
3. *South Wales Evening Post*, 21 June 1912.
4. *Western Mail*, 22 June 1912.
5. A.K.Hignell, *100 First-Class Umpires* (Tempus Publishing, 2003).
6. *South Wales Evening Post*, 8 July 1914.
8. *Western Mail*, 13 July 1914.

Chapter Four
Local rivalries

Few would disagree with the proud boast of a Swansea club official, quoted in *The Cambrian* newspaper during 1878, that "Swansea possesses perhaps the finest cricket facilities of any club in South Wales."[1] Cardiff were probably the only club to match their facilities, having exclusive access at a peppercorn rate from 1867 of a plot of land owned by the Marquess of Bute at the Arms Park. In contrast to the bricks and mortar, plus the industrial landscape which surrounded Cardiff Arms Park, St. Helen's had a far more attractive setting, on the rural-urban fringe of the town and with a maritime outlook.

Thanks to the efforts of the Bancroft family, the practice facilities could more than match those of other club grounds, and a measure of the high standing of the Swansea club can be gained from the fact that they were one of the inaugural participants in the South Wales Cricket Challenge Cup, created in 1879 by the South Wales CC in a bid to match the Rugby Challenge Cup which had been established by their winter rivals, the South Wales Football Union. Cardiff, Carmarthen, Llanelly, Brecon, Newport, Cadoxton, Llandovery College and Canton were the other participants in a competition whose rather cumbersome rules called for the opening round of games to be played on neutral grounds.

Three of the first round ties were in 1879 staged at St. Helen's, giving further evidence of the venue's high standing, with the match between Llandovery College and Newport also witnessing an outstanding all-round performance by CP Lewis, who made an unbeaten 42 in the College's total of 55 before claiming six wickets for just four runs - all clean bowled - as the Newport men were dismissed for just six.

Swansea were drawn against Canton, an up and coming club based in the western suburbs of Cardiff with the game taking place in the grounds of Merthyr Mawr and close to the spacious country home of old Etonian, John Nicholl, the son of the Conservative MP for Cardiff who besides being a leading member of the Bridgend club was a good friend of JTD's. It proved to be an eventful game with Canton making 83 and then reducing Swansea to 37-7, before a late rally by the men from St. Helen's saw them home.

Swansea's participation ended however, much to their chagrin, in the quarter-final against Cardiff, staged at the Arms Park. Batting first the home side amassed 188 with several batsmen benefitting from a series of mis-fields by the visitors. Swansea were then dismissed for 49 in reply with Ben Jones, an employee of the Bute Estate, and a crafty spin bowler, claiming 7/32 as Cardiff secured a place in the semi-finals.

Swansea also departed at the quarter-final stages in 1880 having defeated Llanelli in the opening round. This time a more relaxed approach to choice of venues saw the contest take place at St. Helen's. The *South Wales Daily News* reported how "the field was in capital order" but the wicket was not to the liking of the batsmen from Carmarthenshire with only one getting into double figures as they were dismissed for 76, before the Swansea men knocked off the winning runs.

The visit to Cardiff on 10 July ended again in defeat for Swansea, and on a wet and windy day which was more suited to rugby than cricket. The conditions though did not affect John Price Jones, a leading architect in the town with the man who eight years later helped to convene the meeting at The Angel Hotel which led to the creation of Glamorgan CCC, top-scoring with 36 as Cardiff ended on 111, before dismissing the visitors for 45.

Swansea CC as senn during the late 1890s and in front of the St. Helen's pavilion. Billy Bancroft is seated second left. David Gwynn, the Welsh rugby international, is the umpire standing far right.

Their defeat in the Challenge Cup was the second piece of bad news that summer for the Swansea officials as their prestigious two-day match on 4 and 5 June against the Gentlemen of Canada had been cancelled on the eve of the match. The Canadians had organised matches at both Swansea and Cardiff, after matches in Scotland and Yorkshire. But on the day before the game at St. Helen's, the manager of the touring team sent a telegram to the Swansea secretary from Leicester, saying that the early matches on the tour had been financial disasters and that an advance of £15 would be needed if the two games in South Wales were to go ahead.

It later transpired that their captain, a Yorkshireman called Tom Dale, had been arrested having deserted from the Royal Horse Guards in November 1872. All of the tourists' money had gone with him, and with the Welsh officials unable at such short notice to meet their request, the two matches on Welsh soil were cancelled, with the Canadians heading instead to London for more lucrative games at Lord's and Crystal Palace.

But the embarrassment caused by the late cancellation of the match against the Canadians was only a minor blip for a sporting Club that was really on the up. During the summer months, the nets were full on most weekday evenings as the young men and boys practised their skills under the watchful eye of the Bancrofts, whilst on the half days, the field staged two matches side-by-side as junior teams from the locality used the splendid facilities.

The football section was also going from strength to strength having been founded during 1872. Having initially played under association rules, an informal meeting at the Tenby Hotel in mid-October 1874, saw a group of key figures propose a switch to rugby union. Five days later, the Club officials rubber-stamped the proposals and soon afterwards the first game was staged at Bryn-y-Mor, with several of the leading cricketers also showing talent at the oval-ball game, including Fred Meager and Charlie Chambers.

Above and Below: Rugby at St. Helen's in 1902 and 1903.

After the loss of the Bryn-y-Mor field, the rugby section decamped for 1874/75 and 1875/76 to Primrose Field, the home of the Swansea Workingmen's Club and Institute which had been created during the 1870s by Pascoe St Leger Grenfell, a prominent businessman from Kilvey. With such a well-known local cricketer as their President, it was no surprise that from 1876 the Club were staging cricket matches as well at rugby on Primrose Field. Their leading performer in both codes was Bill Gwynn, who at the time was a teacher at Swansea Parochial School, with his batting and cunning off-spin seeing the Club secure a series of victories besides acting as a flagship for the Club's activities. By 1879, the Club had 131 members with the Treasurer paying tribute to Gwynn's efforts on the cricket field by saying:

> "Many gentlemen have enrolled themselves in the Institution during the past year through its instrumentality."[2]

Buoyed by their success against local teams, and an ever-growing membership, they accepted an offer to play in the South Wales Challenge Cup in 1880, defeating Rhymney in the first round before losing to Christ College, Brecon in the second round. The following year they reached the final, but this was only after beating Penarth in the first round and then having some good fortune to receive byes in the quarter- and semi-final. The Club were fortunate to secure the use of St. Helen's for the final, against Llandovery College, but the bowling of CP Lewis proved to be too good for them, as bowling straight and full at a decent pace, he claimed 5/9 as the Collegians won the Cup.

On 16 December 1882, CP Lewis also led the Welsh rugby team in their first-ever international on home soil as they met England at St. Helen's, on a rainy and blustery day. A crowd of around 3,000 were present as Lewis played in the scarlet jersey of Wales alongside David Gwynn, the star local sportsman, plus Frank Purdon and George Morris who were fellow members of the Swansea rugby club.

The game though was one-sided in favour of the English side who won by two goals and four tries to nil, as the Welsh side, so used to a more aggressive and muscular form of play with a forwards-dominated style with mauls and rucks, were run off their feet by a new style system of three-quarters play, led by the powerful running wing Gregory Wade of Richmond. In the words of the *South Wales Daily News*:

> "the passing of the (English) backs was brilliant in the extreme and the Welshmen appeared quite undone. The home team were all of a heap defending their goal as every opening was invaded. Every weak point was tested by the Englishmen, and but for a short time, the Welshmen managed to keep them back… Lewis eventually got a run but soon lost the ball and ere long, the wonderful passing of the visitors proved too much for the home side".[3]

By the time of this defeat, the Swansea cricketers had reached the first of several appearances in the Challenge Cup. For 1882 the format changed to a regional one, with a western and eastern division using the River Neath as the boundary. However, Cadoxton was included in the east in order to balance the books and after beating Cardiff and Newport, the two crack teams in the east, they met Swansea in the final, held once again at St. Helen's over two weekends in September. Perhaps, though, it was too late in the season as the legacy of rain resulted in damp, bowler friendly conditions, much to the liking of Lewis Jenkins and Lewis Kempthorne as chasing a target of 153, Cadoxton skittled out Swansea for 49.

Swansea made the final again in 1883, defeating Morriston and Llanelli, before heading to Cardiff and hoping for better luck than before in finals at the Arms Park. After a delayed start because of rain, Swansea made 100. Cardiff then gained a slender first innings lead by making 126, before rain interrupted play again with Swansea on 85-5. The Cardiffians immediately claimed a victory on the strength of having a first innings lead, but the men from Swansea disagreed, pointing out the competition rules which stated that all innings should be played out and, after a heated discussion, a replay took place a fortnight later at the Arms Park.

This time Swansea fared much better in their first innings, making 84 before dismissing Cardiff for 46 with Bill Gwynn claiming five wickets. Batting for a second time, Swansea extended their lead to 95 prior to John Price Jones and Tom Barlow making a breezy start against the Swansea seamers before struggling yet again up against Gwynn. The off-spinner made steady inroads yet again and guided Swansea to a 22-run victory. It prompted great joy in the west, especially after the high-handed way in which Cardiff's officials had tried to bend the rules and ecstatic celebrations took place that night in Swansea, as described by the correspondent of the *South Wales Daily News*:

> "placards were posted about the town announcing the result and crowds of devotees awaited the arrival of the team by the 8.20 [p.m.] train. A band played 'See the Conquering Hero Come' as the train entered the station and Bertie Perkins [the captain], Gwynn and Addie were carried on the shoulders of some of their admirers. The band headed the impromptu procession which filled a good portion of High Street and loud cheers greeted the team on all sides."[4]

Celebrations went on long into the night in the Mackworth Arms, with neutral umpire George Rosser from Newport, opting to head west rather than returning home after play! He duly joined in the party and, just for good measure, spent a couple of days relaxing with friends in the Mumbles afterwards.

Cardiff and Swansea met again in the final in 1884 with the team from the east eager to make amends for what had taken place the year before. But the officials from Swansea won the toss to decide the location of the final and, this time, it was the Cardiffians who headed to St. Helen's for the final in August. After winning the toss and opting to bowl, the Cardiff bowlers reduced Swansea to 220 before Matthew Richards, a well-known local barrister and football Blue with Cambridge, made an unbeaten 103.

Rain then twice interrupted Cardiff's reply before reaching 199-8 when

A view from an Edwardian postcard of the St. Helen's ground from Town Hill.

another deluge swept in from Swansea Bay and prevented any further play. Once again a re-match was arranged a fortnight later, but the date was not ideal from the point of view of the Swansea club with several players unavailable through rugby commitments or holidays. The last thing the officials from St. Helen's wanted after the ill feeling the previous year was for Cardiff to be able to gloat over an easy victory against a weak Swansea XI, so rather than sending what amounted to virtually a 2nd XI for a thrashing at the Arms Park, they opted not to send a side at all, and to try and salvage a small measure of pride out of the situation. Cardiff were delighted to win the Cup, but Swansea's actions rankled several of the Cardiff officials and the animosity between east and west continued for several years, with a tit-for-tat action the following summer when Cardiff failed to send a side down to Swansea for their fixture in August.

But this was nothing compared with the acrimony in the Challenge Cup match when Swansea met Morriston at St. Helen's in 1886. The home side had difficulty in raising a team, and at noon the game eventually began but the hour's delay greatly annoyed the visiting side. A second difference of opinion then occurred over the timings for lunch. As reported in *The Cambrian* newspaper:

> "it was discovered that Edgar Reid [a local doctor], who was one of the not out batsmen, was not on the field or prepared to take his place at the wicket. The Morristonians now had a fixed idea that their opponents, having three of their good players absent, were determined to make an effort to obtain a drawn game, and play again with a better team."[5]

Annoyed at the time-wasting tactics, the Morriston team then took their place in the field, without Reid being present, and the ball was put in play. The Morriston wicketkeeper then removed the bails of the unguarded wicket, and the umpire raised his finger to give Reid 'timed out'. A furious row duly broke out as the match abandoned with Swansea on 48-5, with the home batsmen claiming that Dr. Reid, who had quickly returned to his practice, had not been told that the lunch interval had been reduced to half an hour rather than the usual forty-five minutes.

The row continued in the letters page of the *Swansea Herald* newspaper with some of the Swansea members complaining about the partisan behaviour of the Morriston supporters. A correspondent wrote how:

> "the downfall of each Swansea wicket was greeted with yells of delight, whilst any good form shown by the batsmen was observed with chilling silence. Then, when the dispute arose, they flocked to the pavilion and gave vent to their feelings in language far more forcible than polite, applied the grossest epithet to the Swansea men, and demanded that their entrance money should be refunded."[6]

Further letters subsequently appeared from the Morriston lobby criticising the time wasting tactics of the Swansea team, followed by retorts from the latter about the hasty decision of the Morriston team in removing the bails. As the Editor of the *Swansea Herald* subsequently wrote "there was wrong on both sides - Swansea for not turning up before they did and Morrison for being too hasty."[7] The upshot of the dispute was that Swansea withdrew from the competition, with Morriston going on to win the Cup, defeating Llwynypia in the final.

This ugly spat proved to be an unglamorous end to Swansea's participation in the competition as 1886 proved to be the last year of the Cup as the officials of the South Wales CC would up their organisation at their AGM and laid instead the foundations for a proper county organisation. Within three years of this local in-fighting the cricketing community of west Glamorgan united to support Glamorgan as they entered the world of county cricket.

1. *The Cambrian*, 17 May 1878.
2. *South Wales Daily News*, 1 August 1879.
3. *South Wales Daily News*, 18 December 1882.
4. *South Wales Daily News*, 17 September 1883.
5. *The Cambrian*, 20 August 1886. Dr Reid also played rugby for Swansea, whilst his son J.S. died whilst serving in the Great War during 1917 and is one of the people listed on the Club's memorial plaque at St. helen's.
6. *Swansea Herald*, 18 August 1886.
7. *Swansea Herald*, 25 August 1886.

Chapter Five

Swansea becomes a county ground

After several years of acrimony and ill-feeling created by the South Wales Challenge Cup, the cricketers of the region came together in 1888 as the recently knighted JTD Llewelyn convened the meeting at The Angel Hotel in Cardiff with the express purpose of creating a county team which would represent the region and, one day, in the words of JTD "fly at a higher stage" by bringing international cricket to Wales.[1]

As President of the Welsh Rugby Union, it had irked JTD that rugby - a team sport which in many places had grown out of cricket teams - had caught the public's imagination, and after the failure of earlier attempts to form a county team, the squire of Penllergaer was at the forefront of attempts to create a Glamorgan side.

JTD had the fulsome support of William Bryant, the secretary of the Swansea club as well as John Price Jones who with the bat had done much, often at Swansea's expense, to establish Cardiff as the region's pre-eminent club and as a member of the town's mercantile *bourgeoise* he was also eager to see the coal metropolis build on its economic standing by further consolidating its recreational facilities. Other members of the Cardiff club promised support, but the new club was not just "Cardiffshire" as the County's initial committee included representatives from clubs all around the region whilst the team for the first match, in June 1889 at the Arms Park against Warwickshire was also fairly representative of the area's amateur talent.

All of the home games in year one were staged at the Arms Park with Swansea entering the picture in June 1890, when the county met the MCC in a two-day fixture at St. Helen's. The Glamorgan side included estate agent Astley Samuel from the home club, but the latter's selection had its downside as, after being there for the pre-match practice, he had to nip back to work and missed his chance to bat! Also in the Welsh county's team was Bill Gwynn, the captain of both the town's cricket and rugby team, and a man who during the early 1890s subsequently mixed his teaching duties with an administrative role with the Welsh Rugby Union, serving as its first paid secretary from 1892 and acting as Wales' representative on the International Rugby Football Board.

Sadly, he suffered a stroke in 1895 with paralysis preventing him from continuing his teaching duties. Early in 1897, his situation deteriorated as he slipped in and out of a coma and with, in the words of *The Cambrian* newspaper, "his mind being deranged, he was taken to the Bridgend Asylum closer to where his brother and other family members lived" Sadly, he died on 1 April with his funeral in Swansea being attended by the great and the good of sport in South Wales.[2]

Bill's death had been a tragic prelude to Glamorgan's inaugural summer as a Minor County, with the Club's first win duly coming at Swansea during July 1897, and all by the mammoth margin of 233 runs. It was a contest which also saw two other records being created as in their second innings, Cornwall were dismissed for 25 – still the lowest total ever made in any match against Glamorgan – whilst in Cornwall's first innings, Sam Lowe, the Cardiff professional took the first hat-trick recorded by a Glamorgan bowler.

Lowe was a thirty-year old seam bowler who had had a brief career with Nottinghamshire, appearing for his native county once in 1894. He subsequently joined Cardiff and acted as groundsman-professional at the Arms Park until 1906. His younger brother Richard followed him to South Wales and was also in the Glamorgan side for this match with Cornwall. He too had first-class experience with Nottinghamshire and Sussex, and together with his brother held a regular place in the Glamorgan side until the early 1900s. Sam Lowe could be quite a hostile bowler, even on the slow St. Helen's wicket, and his hat-trick against Cornwall in 1897 was described as follows by a local newspaper:

> "[Sam] Hosking, who had laboured for twenty minutes for just one was caught in the slips off Lowe, who had had downright bad luck to date. But with his next ball, the Cardiff bowler knocked over the middle stump of [Philip] Colville Smith, the Cornwall captain, and with his next, he bowled [Christopher] Trevarthen, so performing the hat-trick and gaining unstinted applause from the small band of spectators who had gathered at the St. Helen's ground."[3]

Glamorgan had batted disappointingly in their first innings, but Lowe's spirited efforts helped Glamorgan to an 11-run lead. They fared much better in their second innings with Billy Bancroft and Bertie Letcher each making attractive fifties during a century partnership for the second wicket. Both eventually fell to Jesse Hide, who finished the match with fourteen victims.

As a result of Hide's excellent bowling, Cornwall were left a target of 259 in the three hours and twenty minutes that remained. It seemed a reasonable target, but they collapsed in dramatic fashion within the space of just three-quarters of an hour, and were bowled out for a paltry 25. Sam Lowe and William Lambert both took five wickets, and, along with the rest of Jack Brain's side, they were given a standing ovation as they left the field by the home crowd, few of whom could quite believe how easily and quickly Glamorgan had achieved their first win in the Minor County Championship.

Whilst Billy Bancroft played a passive role in this particular victory, he took centre-stage in other victories by Glamorgan over Minor County opposition. For example, in 1899 he enjoyed a fine game against Surrey 2nd XI, scoring 102, and taking a career-best 5/20 with his seam bowling. In the course of the next four years, In the years leading up to the Great War,

Billy succeeded his father as groundsman at St. Helen's, and then during the inter-war era, Billy turned his attention to coaching, painstakingly passing on many tips to a host of promising young players in the Swansea area, including Gilbert Parkhouse, who duly went on to play Test cricket for England.

In later life, Billy also acted as a match-day steward at the St. Helen's ground when Glamorgan were playing their fixtures at the Swansea ground, always smartly turned out in suit and tie, and with a flower in his button hole. For many years, he proudly sat at the foot of the steps leading up to pavilion, opening and closing the gate as batsmen made their way out to bat on the turf which for so many years he and other members of his family had tended.

Billy died in 1959 and during his life he witnessed a host of changes to the facilities at the ground. During his playing days, he had used the small single-storey pavilion dating from the early 1870s which stood on the northern side of the ground near the entrance from King Edward Road and The Cricketer's Inn. As Jack Morgan recalled, it was chock-a-block of memorabilia celebrating the totemic games during the winter and summer, as well as the feats of Billy and his family:

> "It was a treasure-house of greatness in the sporting life of South Wales. Pity it could not be preserved and given an honoured place in the Welsh National Museum as an inspiration to the youngsters of today, and as a permanent memento of the glorious past..."

Swansea CC 1905 with Billy Bancroft seated first left on the second row, typically with a cigarette this time in his mouth (see p.29 when it was in his hand).

> "In my schoolboy days, every boy had a feeling of awe when he passed the old Swansea cricket pavilion. It was one of the most historic institutions in the town. How we used to dodge Old Man Tucker, the groundsman, but reflecting I now suspect that he very often conveniently had a job out of sight when the boys climbed the low white-washed walls of St. Helen's on big match occasions."[4]

As the evocative mastheads on the county's scorecards illustrate, the single-storey structure was still in use in 1921 as Glamorgan entered the first-class world, with Glamorgan playing host to Warwick Armstrong and the Australian tourists. It was all change by the time the Australians played in Swansea in 1930, as the previous winter had seen the creation of a more spacious building plus tiered seating and the legendary seventy-odd step-walk back up from the playing area and into the dressing rooms. The new building, designed for use by the rugby players and cricketers had seen the creation of two changing rooms plus an umpires room on the ground floor, with separate entrances for the amateurs and professionals, whilst the upper floor contained a colonnade and veranda.

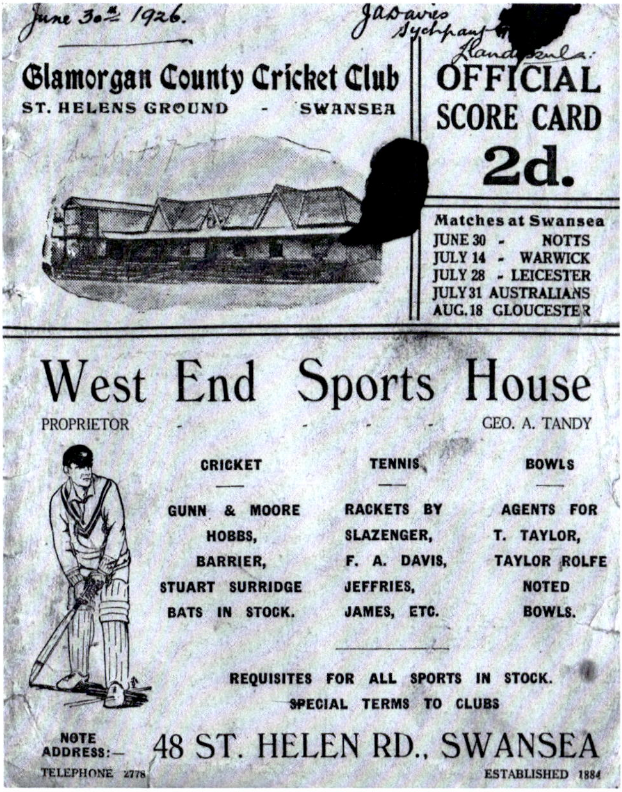

The front cover of a Glamorgan CCC scorecard in 1926.

The impressive new Pavilion, created after construction work during 1929/30.

Improved facilities were also created for the team of groundsmen who looked after the cricket square and rugby pitch. They were led by Harry Creber, the left-arm spinner, who had moved from Liverpool in 1898 to accept a post with the Swansea club, and remained at St. Helen's until his death in 1939. He also became a stalwart in Glamorgan's Minor County side and in 1905 became the Club's first-ever bowler to claim over a hundred wickets in a season. During the season, his wickets cost 15 runs apiece, with returns of 13/82 against Wiltshire at Chippenham and 11/148 in the match with the MCC at Cardiff Arms Park.

He repeated the feat in 1906 with 112 victims at 13 runs apiece, and during the 1908 match with Carmarthenshire, he came agonisingly close to becoming the first Glamorgan player to take all ten wickets in an innings. In the end, Creber finished with career-best figures of 9/56 and completely baffled the inexperienced Carmarthenshire batsmen. Creber was past his best by the time Glamorgan were elevated to the County Championship, but he still managed to claim 95 wickets, albeit at the cost of 26 apiece, and all at the age of 50!

After retiring from playing, Creber also became a well-known bird fancier, and won many prizes at shows with his Yorkshire canaries. A man renowned for his stoicism, he never wore an overcoat whilst tending the ground, even on the coldest of winter days and when the All Whites were playing on the rugby ground, Harry would always be in shirt-sleeves with his shirt open at the neck.

Harry died at his home in the Uplands on 27 March 1939, and one can only imagine what the stalwart of sport at St. Helen's would have said as the war clouds loomed yet again, bringing an end for many the happy days of

Harry Creber.

watching or playing cricket and rugby at the ground overlooking Swansea Bay. With the declaration of war with Germany, conscription and no means of honouring the terms of their lease of St. Helen's, Swansea Cricket and Football Club surrendered its tenure of the ground to the Swansea Town Corporation.

It was therefore under their jurisdiction that several changes took place to the pavilion during the winter of 1946/47, ostensibly to maintain international rugby in Swansea and to increase the amount of terracing where people could sit to watch the matches. The result was that the concrete banking was extended, virtually obscuring the ground floor of the pavilion, whilst the upper floor was enlarged to include a new bar and seating area, whilst on the roof four turret-like pagodas were created with the front two being used by the scorers and journalists.

Indeed, there are many tales, some no doubt apocryphal, of this being the location where John Arlott and Welsh poet Dylan Thomas met up and shared a bottle or three of the finest red wine as they watched a series of games in 1948 as Wilf Wooller's team moved closer and closer to the Championship title.

There are no surviving records to show that the pair were present for the three-day match at St. Helen's starting on 15 September against a South of England XI as the Welsh county staged a festival week of cricket in Swansea and Cardiff to celebrate their first Championship title. But Billy Bancroft was there, proudly sporting a daffodil in his lapel as he manned the player's gate back up to the pavilion.

Billy was hoping that his prodigy Gilbert Parkhouse could showcase his talents in this match against some of the finest players in southern

England, but it was not to be as Gilbert was dismissed for 0 and 1. However, the game had a happy ending as far as the locals were concerned as, set a target of 250 on the final afternoon, Allan Watkins, happily restored to full fitness after an injury sustained during the closing Ashes Test, made an unbeaten 111 to see the Welsh county secure a two-wicket victory.

The Swansea ground during the late 1920s,
and prior to the installation of the raised seating lining Gorse Lane.

1. *Western Mail*, 7 July 1889.
2. *South Wales Evening Post*, 27 February 1897.
3. *South Wales Daily News*, 25 July, 1897.
4. J.H.Morgan, *Glamorgan County Cricket* (Convoy Publications, 1952).

Chapter Six

Swansea at war

The summer of 1914 had begun for the cricketers of the Swansea club no differently to those years which had gone before. It seemed to be very much a case of business as normal as on the first Saturday in May, the town club staged a trial match at St. Helen's before the following week they defeated Neath after a century from James Maxwell, their talented all-rounder who had previously played first-class cricket for Somerset, and who had been a regular for several summers in the Glamorgan side.

In mid-May, the ground overlooking Swansea Bay witnessed a keenly fought match against Briton Ferry Town. At first Swansea's batsmen were in trouble against the accurate off-cutters of Jack Johns, who caught and bowled Edgar Billings, the free-scoring wicketkeeper who played regularly for Glamorgan before Johns also caught Billy Bancroft. Swansea eventually mustered 139 but Briton Ferry's hopes of victory were dashed towards the end of the home team's innings as Eddie Bates, the ex-Yorkshire professional, badly dislocated a finger and departed the ground for medical attention. Without their crack batsman, they struggled against the nagging accuracy of spinner Harry Creber and the lively seam bowling of Maxwell, and they were bundled out for just 50 with the former claiming 5/18.

James Maxwell.

Swansea's decent run of form came to an abrupt end at the end of the month at Stradey Park, as Ernie Gee, a schoolmaster at Gowerton County School, took 7/51 before Percy Rees and Claude Warner shared a vibrant opening stand as Llanelli took just over an hour to reach the modest total of 112. A few days later, Swansea hosted The Bath and West Show, and despite heavy showers, a large crowd turned out at St. Helen's to watch the various equestrian displays. With their ground in use, the town's cricketers duly headed the following Saturday to Cardiff, but the bowling of Ernie Vost, the former Lancashire and Staffordshire cricketer proved to be too much of a handful as he took 5/30 with Swansea being dismissed for 81.

After their decent early season form, Creber, Maxwell and Bancroft were duly chosen in Glamorgan's side for their opening Minor Counties Championship match against Surrey at The Oval on 1 June, followed two days later by a match at Sunderland against Durham. After drawing against Surrey, Glamorgan's hardy band of amateurs and professionals travelled by train to the North East. The long journey allowed many in the party to catch up on some sleep, though some of the amateurs no doubt opted to read the newspapers, several of which carried photographs of the wedding of Prince Oscar of Prussia, the German Emperor's fifth son to Countess Ida Marie von Vasewitz, a lady-in-waiting to the Empress. As they headed north on the overnight express, few could have imagined how the Kaiser would play such an important role in their lives over the course of the next few months following the assassination on 28 June of Archduke Francis Ferdinand, the heir to the throne of the Austro-Hungarian empire and his wife Sophie, Duchess of Hohenberg.

Whilst matters were escalating in Eastern Europe, Glamorgan had organised a trio of back-to-back county matches at St. Helen's during July 1914, with fixtures against Northamptonshire, Durham and Essex 2nd XI. The first game against the East Midlands county, who had been admitted into the County Championship in 1905, gave the Welsh side a chance to assess their own strength ahead of what the county's committee hoped would be a renewed bid for elevation to first-class status. But after being put in to bat on a damp wicket, Glamorgan's batsmen struggled in their first innings before Harry Creber prospered on his home wicket and kept the visitors in check. After being set 240 in two and a half hours, the Northants batsmen then opted for a safety-first approach as the game petered out into a draw.

The weather interrupted the match with Durham, but the Cardiff pairing of Jock Tait and Norman Riches each posted half-centuries. Neath's Bill Bestwick also shone with the ball together with Creber, and their combined efforts once again saw the visiting batsmen opt against a helter-skelter pursuit of a target of 213 in two and a half hours. In the game against a strong Essex 2nd XI, first honours went to the visiting bowlers, before the Swansea pairing of Percy Morris and Maxwell led a counter-attack. Yet again, Creber spun his way through some modest resistance as Glamorgan secured a decent first innings lead of 93. To the delight of a crowd in excess of a thousand the following morning, Billy Bancroft raced to an

The St. Helen's ground, as seen in 1914.

unbeaten hundred before Essex's batsmen grimly hung on for a draw.

The enthusiasm and joy of Glamorgan's supporters at the excellent form of their side in the matches at Swansea was swiftly tempered by the ever-worsening news in the *South Wales Evening Post.* Reading articles with headlines such as "Europe is in a state of suspense" and "The shadow of war is overhanging" left nobody in any doubt about what was going to unfold. Glamorgan's dreams of first-class status in 1915 or 1916 swiftly evaporated as Britain declared war with Germany in early August and within a couple of weeks, British troops were in action on foreign soil as the First World War began.

One of the first signs in Swansea of the impending hostilities had come in late July as a detachment of two dozen men from the Welch Border Regiment travelled from Pembroke Dock to take up positions guarding the entrance into the town's docks. The August Bank Holiday weekend saw cricket briefly continue and Creber continued in fine form as he bowled Glamorgan to victory over Surrey 2nd XI at the Arms Park. But with war having been declared, and the Great Western Railway now operating an emergency timetable as they attempted to transport troops to various military training camps and ports in southern England, getting safely back home to London, rather than chasing a target of 184, must have been uppermost in the minds of the Surrey players.

By the time that Harry Creber had returned to his home in Swansea, a number of German vessels had already been seized in the town's docks, whilst old soldiers, reservists and territorials were signing up in droves at the recruiting stations. With rumours of a German invasion, there was also some panic buying, with two shops in Swansea having to temporarily close after completely running out of provisions. A few days later when several grocery stores raised their prices, shoppers responded in an angry way by smashing their windows.

Shortly afterwards, Glamorgan announced that their concluding away matches against Wiltshire at Trowbridge and Essex 2nd XI at Leyton plus the game with the MCC at the Arms Park had all been cancelled. Shortly after, Swansea rugby club, who had organised a few trial matches, announced that their forthcoming fixtures had also been cancelled, and the season of 1914 drew to a hasty close at St. Helen's as a couple of benefit matches for Bancroft were arranged against both Llanelli and Cardiff. As further contingents of troops signed up in Swansea, and throughout South Wales, the mood was quite upbeat with most people believing that the war would be over by Christmas. The reality was very, very different and it was not until some five years later that cricket finally resumed.

By September 1914 a series of rifles ranges were established across the outfield at St. Helen's, with the facility being used by the Swansea Battalion Voluntary Training Corps. The cricketers soon swapped their whites for khaki uniform, with James Maxwell, like so many of the town's sportsmen, readily answering Lord Kitchener's call to arms. He enlisted with the Royal Artillery and duly undertook a number of postings in Cyprus, Salonika, Egypt and Palestine. During the latter, he was wounded in both his right arm and leg by flying shrapnel and was forced to return home where his wounds eventually healed. So many others, though, were not so fortunate as they died doing their gallant best for King and Country on the bloody battlefields of France and Belgium.

After being discharged in March 1920, Maxwell returned to Swansea and re-opened his sports outfitters shop and drapery business which he had established a dozen or so years before, following his move from the West Country to South Wales. But whereas several of those who returned from foreign fields were able to resume their cricketing careers, Maxwell's injured arm and leg ruled out any thoughts of resuming his career as a professional cricketer. However, he retained a link with the Swansea club and mixed coaching duties with running his drapery and sports outfitters. He duly met with some success but, for the second time, the Germans had an important say in his life as his premises were completely destroyed by bombing in 1943.

But many others who played at Swansea during 1914 did not return, including David Cuthbert Thomas, the only son of Reverend Evan Thomas, the vicar of Llanedy near Ammanford, who had shown rich promise as a young sportsman at Christ College Brecon. His performances in matches at Brecon and also at St. Helen's had impressed the watching Glamorgan selectors, and in June 1914 after completing a match-winning innings for the school against Builth Wells, the nineteen year-old was chosen in their all-amateur team for the match against their counterparts from Carmarthenshire at Stradey Park in Llanelli on 27 and 28 July in 1914.

Tommy's parents and girlfriend were delighted to travel the short distance from Ammanford to Llanelli to watch the game as the Glamorgan Gentlemen chased a target of 321 to win. Arthur O'Bree, a Colonel in the Territorial Army, led the way with a fluent hundred, and was well past 150 when the young schoolboy went out to bat, eager to continue the good work. But as the target drew near, there was the clatter of wickets. O'Bree departed for 199, whilst Tommy was caught, and although Archie Pritchard, the Swansea fast bowler, used the long handle to strike a couple of lusty blows, he became the final man to depart as Carmarthenshire secured a narrow victory by five runs.

Tommy's nimble and athletic fielding had impressed the watching officials from Glamorgan who were contemplating their teams for further games, but with the country already on a war footing, August 1914 saw Tommy join the Public Schools Battalion, rather than remain in South Wales and take part in further matches of cricket at St. Helen's. He subsequently trained at RMC Sandhurst, before securing a commission as a Second Lieutenant in 7th Infantry Division of the 1st Battalion of the Royal Welch Fusiliers. Also in the Regiment were the famous writers Robert Graves and Siegfried Sassoon, with whom Tommy became close friends. Each wrote poems about the young Welshman with the following being Sassoon's description of their first meeting in May 1915:

> "He had unpacked and arranged his belongings, and was sitting on his camp-bed polishing a perfectly new pipe. He looked up at me. Twilight was falling and there was only one small window, but even in the half-light his face surprised me by its candor and freshness. He had obvious good looks which go with fair hair and firm features, but it was the radiant integrity of his expression which astonished me. While I was getting ready for dinner we exchanged a few remarks. His tone of voice was simple and reassuring, like his appearance. How does he manage to look like that? I thought; and for the moment I felt all my age. His was the bright countenance of truth; ignorant and undoubting; incapable of concealment but strong in reticence and in modesty."[1]

Early in 1916 the Battalion were involved in manoeuvres which were part of the Battle of the Somme, with Tommy and the others enduring bitterly cold temperatures whilst in the trenches. By early March, they were in the vicinity of Fricourt of Picardy and Tommy's mood must have been uplifted by the receipt of a food parcel from his former friends at Christ College. He duly wrote a letter of thanks back to the school, but tragically, it proved to be the last letter he wrote back to Brecon.

On the evening of 18 March, Tommy accompanied a party from C Company out into no-man's land near a building known as The Citadel to check the barbed wire defences, to repair anything that was damaged and to repair any gaps where the Germans had been trying to cut through. This was routine work at night for the Allies, but it was fraught with danger as the Germans were also busy in the dark. If a flare went up the men would remain motionless - instinct was to duck or fall to the ground, but the slightest movement would draw fire from German snipers or from a machine-gun placement. Sometimes they would fire shots at random into the darkness hoping to hit one of their foes.

This was the case that fateful night for Tommy as around 10.30pm he was

DC Thomas (second left) standing with a colleague from Christ College plus two of the Swansea Wednesdays XI whom they played at St. Helen's, Swansea in 1914. In the background of this photograph is the old pavilion at the Bryn Road end of the Swansea ground.

struck in the throat. He was able to make it back to the first-aid station unassisted, and, initially, all seemed well as a dressing was applied by the regimental doctor who was a throat specialist in civilian life. "You'll be all right, only don't raise your head for a bit," said the medic. But the wound began to haemorrhage with Tommy taking a letter to his family and fiancée from his pocket and giving it to an orderly, saying "Post this!". They were the last words he would utter as shortly afterwards he started to choke. The doctor returned and desperately tried a tracheotomy, but it was too late and, shortly afterwards, Tommy died.

Dyson Bransby Williams was another Swansea sportsman to be broken both physically and mentally by the horrors of the Great War. Born in October 1877, he was the third son of civil engineer Morgan Bransby Williams of Killay House – a comfortable house with spacious grounds to the west of the town of Swansea. Cricket was in the Bransby Williams' blood with country house matches taking place in the grounds of his home, whilst his eldest son George created during the late 1880s a team called the Public School Nondescripts as the Bransby Williams boys, together with their well-heeled friends from other well-to-do families in the area, played matches against the leading clubs at both Killay House and St. Helen's.

He also played for Killay in the Swansea and District League and in June 1901 had become the League's first player to win county honours as he played for Glamorgan against Monmouthshire at Rodney Parade. It was to be another eleven years, interrupted by his legal training, before Williams

Dyson Bransby Williams

played again for the county, and by 1912, he had also become the captain of Swansea's 1st XI. Through his friendship with Tom Whittington, the Neath-born solicitor who was Glamorgan's captain, Williams also agreed to succeed Hugh Ingledew, the Welsh rugby international, as Glamorgan's Treasurer as the decision-making powerhouse of Glamorgan CCC shifted west.

Whilst very proud of his achievements in captaining the Swansea club and playing for Glamorgan, Williams was happiest playing in the more relaxed and convivial surroundings of Killay House, especially playing for the Public School Nondescripts. As Jack Morgan later recalled,

> "Dyson Williams, with his panama covering his baldness, was a familiar figure on the cricket field in those days We were engaged in amateur theatricals together and this led to many invitations to play cricket at Killay House, and there is no better way of enjoying the game. Something went out of cricket when those house parties became a diminishing feature in the sporting life of south Wales."[2]

Williams duly became a fine soldier and a popular officer, overseeing the recruitment and training at St. Helen's by the 14th (Swansea Battalion) of the Welch Regiment, and to Williams went much of the credit for its initial formation under Colonel Benson on 16 September, 1914, with Williams himself acting as captain and adjutant. It was no surprise either that Williams swiftly rose to the rank of lieutenant colonel in France, and was to be second-in-command of the Swansea Battalion throughout the war, apart from a six-week period in the autumn of 1918 when he commanded a brigade of the Royal Welsh Fusiliers.

1916 saw Williams and the Swansea Battalion travel to France where they were thrown into the attack on Mametz Wood in which so many Welshmen lost their lives. Williams, himself, was severely wounded advancing up the slope leading to the wood and it was feared that he would die in the ambulance train. For a long period "he lay between life and death", and his actions won him the Military Cross, but this was of little comfort as so many of his comrades and friends lost their lives.

He returned to the battalion in 1917, and subsequently showed outstanding leadership at Ypres, with his regiment going over the top at Pilkem Ridge and routing the crack Prussian "Cockchafers". It was an action which deservedly earned him the DSO. In the same year his "Swansea's" also won high honours in an attack on the salient known as Caesar's Nose, and subsequently figured in the Ancre crossing and the engagements at Auveley Wood and the River Selle.

During the peace negotiations in 1918 Lieutenant Colonel Williams was also chosen to act as a guide to Prime Minister Lloyd George over the Somme battlefield. It was no surprise therefore that in December he succeeded Colonel Brooke to the command of the Swansea Battalion. He was pleased as well to observe the return of sporting activities to St. Helen's with cricket matches during 1918 with games against a number of military teams including the Lancashire Fusiliers as well as Swansea Grammar School, whilst in May 1918 St. Helen's had a well-attended baseball match with teams drawn from personnel representing Canada and their counterparts from the USA. Canada won 13-3.[3]

But the war had taken its toll, and if truth were known, he never fully recovered from the bloody horrors with the man who marched through Swansea at the head of his battalion in June 1919 to present the colours to the Mayor being a very different fellow to the happy and jolly man who had marched off to war five years before.

In July 1919 he was invalided out of the Army, largely as a result of the injury to a lung sustained whilst on the Somme, and he returned to live with his mother and brothers at Killay House. He did not, however, return to the legal profession, and instead engaged in a stock and share business. This failed, as did the Welsh Aviation Company in which he had speculated. He continued to play a bit of cricket and continued to serve as Glamorgan's Treasurer, although his heart was not really in the Club's affairs and he only agreed to carry on to help out his old friend Tom Whittington who was now actively seeking assurances and support from English counties to support Glamorgan's campaign for first-class status

Whittington was fortunate enough in the Autumn of 1920 to secure the minimum of eight home and away fixtures with existing first-class counties, and there was great celebration when the MCC endorsed Glamorgan's application to join the County Championship in 1921. By this time, Williams' best years were behind him but he still managed to make an appearance in first-class cricket, at the ripe old age of 44, as he appeared in the last match of Glamorgan's inaugural County Championship season against Hampshire at Cardiff. He duly made five and nine as Glamorgan, dismissed for 37 and 114, lost by an innings inside two days.

But Williams' mind lay elsewhere and in 1921 had left Swansea to try his luck in London and elsewhere. In particular, he went to live with an old Army comrade, Major Arnold Wilson, who had become a boxing promoter, at his house at Maidenhead. Williams duly became a close friend of the world light-heavyweight champion, Georges Carpentier, with whom he wrote a song with the music penned by Williams under the pseudonym Florian Brock, to the words by Carpentier himself, called "Vagabond Philosophy". It was sub-titled "I'll be all right", and it poignantly included the following lines:

> "And so in life you'll get
> A regular knockout blow.
> Don't lie and grouse, but try to smile
> And have the pluck to cry.
> The mud and dust will soon rub off.
> I'll be all right, by and by."[4]

But Williams' optimism proved to be misplaced, and shortly before the publication of "Vagabond Philosophy" he was declared bankrupt. He vanished for a while after the bankruptcy hearings, with his brother Morgan finding him "in a rather down and out state", he took him to his home in Maidenhead where he stayed for a while. Whilst with his brother, he spoke about his financial problems, attributing the situation to an inadequate Army pay, coupled with the cost of maintaining his law firm during the war. But in truth his betting and gambling, in addition to taking out loans at a heavy interest, had had a crippling effect on his personal situation and these were the real reasons for his predicament.

In late February Williams' world fell in as his mother died. A confirmed bachelor, he told Wilson he felt desolate, and soon afterwards went to Belgium to play the casinos. His behaviour relapsed again as cheques started to bounce, whilst he also deceived the owner of a bar into giving him the sum of £200 for a cheque, which then bounced. His debts to Wilson also mounted, but he was able to write to Wilson saying: "I have at last struck a bit of luck, just when apparently things were hopeless. I shall be able to pay you back what you have let me have."

Wilson received that letter on 19 April. Tragically, the day before, the charlady had gone to clean Wilson's offices in St. Martin's Court in London. She found the room full of gas, with Williams slumped to the floor. The gas stove had two taps fully turned on. The 45 year-old solicitor-soldier-cricketer had become yet another, if belated victim of the war, with the coroner duly recording a verdict of "suicide while of unsound mind".

1. From *The Toll of War - Christ College Brecon, 1914-1918* by Glenn Horridge with Felicity Kilpatrick.
2. J.H.Morgan, *Glamorgan County Cricket* (Convoy Publications, 1952)
3. *South Wales Weekly Post*, 11 May 1918.
4. Article by Bob Harragan in the *Cricket Statistician*, June 1985

Chapter Seven
A place for all seasons

Glamorgan's elevation into first-class cricket saw the St. Helen's ground stage its inaugural County Championship match – and the Welsh county's second – on 28 May, 1921 with Leicestershire visiting Swansea. It saw Ewart Astill, the visiting opener, score 115 as the East Midlands side made 335 on the opening day, before claiming two cheap wickets.

On the second day, Glamorgan were dismissed for 192 before their bowlers dismissed Leicestershire for 70, and buoyed by their efforts, Norman Riches made a fluent start in their pursuit of the target of 214. With Glamorgan having beaten Sussex in their opening game at the Arms Park a fortnight before, a few dreamt of another victory for the Welsh county, but these romantics had their hopes dashed as none of the other batsmen could support the Cardiff batsman and after he departed for 57, Glamorgan ended twenty runs short.

This defeat by Leicestershire was followed later in the summer by innings defeats against Gloucestershire and Somerset, and although Frank Pinch, a Cornish-born schoolmaster scored a century in their victory against Worcestershire, there had been little for Glamorgan's supporters to cheer at Swansea in 1921. Worse was to follow the next year as all five of the county's games at St. Helen's ended in sizeable defeats, with Sussex winning by an innings, Hampshire by 178 runs, Northamptonshire by 103 runs, Derbyshire by 283 runs and Lancashire by an innings.

The losing sequence at Swansea ended in 1923 as victories were recorded against Northamptonshire and Gloucestershire, but the damage had been done during the previous two years with gate receipts at St. Helen's falling, and coupled with the team's poor showing elsewhere, there were calls for Glamorgan to return to the Minor County ranks. The fact that they continued as a first-class county and went on to enjoy much success at the ground overlooking Swansea Bay stemmed from the emergence of a rich seam of young homegrown talent.

Maurice Turnbull was one of these fresh faces to emerge during the 1920s with the man who went on to become a dual international, representing Wales at rugby, besides playing cricket for England and Glamorgan, making his first appearance in Glamorgan's ranks at St. Helen's in 1924. Swansea was a most appropriate location for his first-class debut, given the way he personified the dual nature of the Swansea ground, and it's place in both the winter and summer schedules of sporting activities in South Wales.

It was also the icing on the cake that his highest-ever score for his beloved county should also occur at Swansea in 1937. By the time he made a

The 1921 Australians walk out from the old Swansea pavilion.

glorious double-century against Worcestershire at St. Helen's, Glamorgan were on course to reach seventh place in the county table - their highest-ever in the Championship - whilst the Club's bank balance had been in the black for several summers.

How different it was back in 1924 when the name of MJL Turnbull first appeared on the county's team list with the Club tottering from one game to another like a drunk going from one pub to the next. The deficit of £2,951 at the end of the previous season meant that 1924 saw the Welsh county relying heavily once again on amateurs rather than hiring any extras from the paid ranks. Indeed, the club was run very much on a shoestring budget, with the wives and sisters of the amateurs helping to save money on the catering by making the sandwiches for the professionals lunch, whilst their men-folk did their bit to reduce the club's debt.

By early August 1924, some of the regular professionals were so out of form that the selection committee decided to give them a rest. One of these was Dai Davies, who the year before had made his home debut at Swansea after undertaking a double-shift at the steelworks in Llanelli with the young professional arriving at the St. Helen's ground courtesy of a taxi which had been sent to his home.

Maurice Turnbull was Dai's replacement with the schoolboy fresh from a prolific summer playing for Downside School, the Roman Catholic boarding school south of Bath where the Cardiff-born youngster and his brothers had been sent by their father who was a leading figure in the shipping trade in the coal metropolis. His call-up came for the match at St. Helen's against Lancashire, one of the strongest teams at the time in the County Championship, and the day before the match at Swansea, Maurice joined the other players in the nets at the Arms Park.

Maurice Turnbull displaying his batting talents off the front foot.

As Johnnie Clay, the Glamorgan captain, later remembered:

> "Maurice was not really looking the part. He was so nervous and did so badly that he suggested that it might be best after all if he did not play against Lancashire. Luckily for him and for Glamorgan, I took him to one side and was able to talk him out of standing down, telling him some nonsense about the actors who had told me that a bad dress rehearsal guaranteed a successful first night!"[2]

Later in the day, Maurice and his father travelled by train to Swansea, primarily to allow the youngster to get a good night's sleep in a hotel before his big day. As it happened, Maurice did not have the greatest of rests, but it was certainly more than the Lancashire team who arrived at St. Helen's in a quite weary state on the morning of 13 August, after having travelled by overnight train from Blackpool. Johnnie Clay was delighted to see the visitor's many yawns as they knocked up on the morning of the match so after winning the toss, he had little hesitation in batting first, believing that their long journey would hamper the Lancashire attack.

It proved not to be and when Maurice walked out to bat, the scoreboard was reading 24-4. But the fresh-faced youngster looked more like a seasoned professional with over a hundred appearances under his belt as he calmly played himself in and helped to rectify the situation. As Nomad wrote in the *Western Mail*:

> "from the moment he came in, he batted with the assurance, coolness and judgement of a veteran and in 35 minutes before lunch obtained

> nine runs in good style. After the resumption, he settled back in quickly and played in textbook manner. For ninety minutes, the express deliveries of [Ted] McDonald, the cunning slows of [Dick] Tyldesley and the subtle and varied deliveries of [Cec] Parkin were all played by this young lad with skill and confidence."[3]

With some delicate late cuts and leg glides, he reached 40 in faultless style before being deceived by a top spinner from Dick Tyldesley and trapped leg before. His efforts had helped Glamorgan to a more respectable total of 153. Professionals Helm Spencer and Frank Ryan then gave the Welsh county an unexpected but most well deserved lead of two runs before heavy rain on the second morning washed out play.

When spectators gathered in front of the Swansea pavilion in glorious sunshine on the final morning of the match, they were keeping their fingers crossed that the home batsmen would not subside as meekly as they had in previous games that summer. The portents did not look good as within the first hour, Glamorgan collapsed to 28-4 leading some spectators, who were fearing the worst, to head across the Oystermouth Road to the adjacent station on the Mumbles Railway and going somewhere else on the steam-hauled trains for their afternoon entertainment.

Those who stayed were richly rewarded for their patience and loyalty as for the second time in the game, the schoolboy and Trevor Arnott steadied the ship. After being impressed with Maurice's strokeplay in the first innings, 'Nomad' was now impressed by his watchful defense, writing how "Turnbull watches the ball right onto his bat and this together with apparently inexhaustible patience was the secret of his success."

He had been at the wicket for exactly an hour, making a calm 16, before he got a spiteful ball from Parkin and was adjudged leg before for the second time in the match. A few wags in the crowd started to suggest that Turnbull's demise signalled the end of Glamorgan's resistance, but Jack Mercer, the jovial seam bowler and hard-hitting lower order batsman duly played a little gem of an innings as in twenty minutes he hit a valiant 36 with a mix of well timed drives and lusty slogs.

By the time Mercer was dismissed, Lancashire had a target of 146 and most of the afternoon in which to chase the target. Harry Makepeace and Ernest Tyldesley gave the Northern side a solid start and on 84-3 they appeared to have the measure of the bowling. With Lancashire seemingly coasting towards victory, Johnnie Clay sauntered over to Frank Ryan, and said to the irascible spinner "Right, Frank. It's now or never!" Much to Johnnie's delight, he responded with one of the finest ever spells of his career, taking 7/23 and, with Lancashire falling 39 runs short of their target, Jack Morgan wrote:

> "the Lancashire batsmen must have thought they were in the coils of a serpent. Bringing the ball down from his fine height, Ryan spun it like a top on the dusty surface, and batsman after batsman groped and lunged in vain as the ball spun wickedly passed their bats."[4]

When the last wicket fell, Ryan was carried shoulder high off the field by the fellow professionals, and much merry-making then followed to celebrate the finest-ever Championship victory Glamorgan had ever recorded on Swansea soil. A flood of tributes were duly paid in the newspapers about the remarkable batting of the 18 year-old who was still at Downside School, and having kept his place in the side for the next match, against Somerset at Cardiff, he took the opportunity to sit in the Arms Park pavilion and write to Father Sigebert, the Headmaster of Downside about his experiences in the victory against Lancashire match:

> "The three days were just wonderful: every bit of the cricket was ripping. Press notices, snapshots and autograph signing were not quite so ripping, still there is a certain glamour attached even to these. The result of it all is that I am frightfully proud of myself - nearly as proud as my father is. The pity of it is that it probably won't last. It seems one has to have luck to make runs unless one is very good. The bowling especially that of Parkin, fully confirmed my worst fears - I usually knew something about three balls per over - sometimes less. Both sides took their cricket light heartedly when not actually engaged upon it. One o'clock was my earliest time for bed. The amateurs did things in a bunch together."[5]

Maurice Turnbull seen at Swansea in 1937.

This was the first of 70 appearances in first-class cricket which Maurice made at St. Helen's, in addition to over two dozen games during the winter months when playing rugby for Cardiff and Glamorgan, as well as appearing for the Probables or Possibles in Final Welsh Trials held at the Swansea ground. As Maurice wrote in an article for *The Catholic Times*, playing rugby at St. Helen's was a far more intimidating experience than playing cricket:

> "There are many other changing rooms where I have been sat before a game, and nearly deafened by the noise made by spectators stamping their feet and cheering in the enclosures above. But when playing against Swansea you also ran the gauntlet, sprinting out from the changing rooms and onto the pitch, as people swore and even sometimes spat at you, whilst some women even waived their umbrellas in your direction. I especially remember one very partisan young lady from Swansea who almost hit me, yet a week or so later when I was playing at St. Helen's in a Welsh trial, she was standing there loudly cheering and applauding me. How fickle supporters can be!"[6]

A number of other Glamorgan cricketers appeared in these rugby matches, as well as the internationals which continued to be held at the ground until the early 1950s. On 10 March 1934, Viv Jenkins, who appeared in 44 matches for Glamorgan, became the first full-back to score a try for Wales as they defeated Ireland 13-10 at St. Helen's. Four years later, Wilf Wooller was also in the Welsh side which defeated Ireland 11-5. This was one of eighteen caps the sporting all-rounder made for Wales, with the first coming against England in 1932/33 and, whilst still a pupil at Rydal School, he wrote his name into his country's sporting folklore as he became a member of the first Welsh side to win at Twickenham.

It followed an outstanding performance at outside centre for the Possibles in the Final Welsh Trial at Swansea on 7 January, with Wilf becoming the first North Walian to be chosen for forty years. He travelled alone by train down to Swansea and, as Wilf later recalled:

> "It was quite an adventure to say the least as I had never been down to the south before, and as the steam train sped through the countryside of mid Wales, I sat quietly in a compartment gazing out of the window at the new scenery. As the train headed south, I was joined by two men who engaged in earnest conversation about the state of Welsh rugby and the likely side for the home internationals. To my amazement, they got out a copy of the *Western Mail* and started discussing the merits of each player named in the newspaper to appear in the trial at Swansea..."
>
> "After going through the forwards and half-becks, one turned to the other and said 'Who's this Wooller from up North? There was a shrug of the shoulders from his friend.'Dunno' was the eventual reply... I tried to hide my embarrassment at being talked about by total strangers. It was almost getting too much but they eventually got off the train,

leaving me to carry on the journey and reflect on the way the game aroused deep passion and serious discussion."[7]

Wilf also played a starring role in Wales' victory over the 1935 All Blacks at Cardiff Arms Park. It was not a successful time in South Wales that year for the New Zealanders as earlier in the tour they were beaten 11-3 by the All Whites at St. Helen's. This was not the first time Swansea had defeated an international touring team as on Boxing Day 1908 they had defeated Australia 6-0, whilst four years later to the day they beat South Africa 3–0.

Swansea's victory in 1935 made them the first Welsh club to beat the big three nations from the Southern Hemisphere, and what made that day even more special was the fact that Swansea's half-backs were two fresh-faced youngsters, Willie Davies and Haydn Tanner from Gowerton County School. Their match-winning partnership prompted the immortal comment to visiting journalists by Jack Manchester, the captain of The All Blacks – "Tell them that we have been beaten, but please don't tell them that it was by a pair of schoolboys!"[8]

A line-out from a rugby match at Swansea in 1903. Note the dress, and position of the referee, plus the old pavilion in the background at the Bryn Road end. The skyline is therefore very different compared with the backdrop in the photo opposite.

1. A.K.Hignell, *Maurice Turnbull: A Welsh Sporting Hero* (Tempus Publishing, 2001)
2. Ibid.
3. *Western Mail*, 14 August 1924.
4. J.H.Morgan, *Glamorgan County Cricket* (Convoy Publications, 1952).
5. A.K.Hignell op.cit
6. Ibid
7. A.K.Hignell, *The Skipper: A biography of Wilf Wooller* (Limlow Book, 1995)
8. *South Wales Evening Post*, 29 September 1935

Chapter Eight

Swansea-by-the-sea

The distinctive nature of the St Helen's ground, overlooking Swansea Bay, has made it a favourable place over the years for bowlers, especially those who swing the ball around. There have been many occasions in Glamorgan's history - if all the elements are in the right place - with the tide coming in plus a decent amount of cloud overhead, the swing bowlers have prospered.

Some have claimed that the pitch actually changes colour with the incoming tide, but this may be part of the mythology and mystique of county cricket's seaside venue with long-serving groundsman George Clement instead noticing that when the tide moved in, it brought a salty sea breeze which caused his spectacles to mist up.[1] In his estimation, it was these damp breezes which made the ball move in the air and off the seam, and explained why several Glamorgan captains including Wilfred Wooller would consult the local tide tables before deciding whether it would be best to bat or bowl first when winning the toss.

The legendary microclimate however has not always helped the home side, perhaps most famously in their Gillette Cup match in June 1974

Wilf Wooller inspects the Swansea wicket with, to the right, long-serving groundsman George Clement.

against Lincolnshire when the decision to bat first back-fired on the Welsh county as they slumped to 59-8 with the swing and seam of Martin Maslin and Terry Barnes being almost unplayable at times. Glamorgan's plight however was not helped by some ill-advised blows against the canny left-arm spin of John Dale.

Tony Cordle and Malcolm Nash partially spared Glamorgan's blushes with a ninth wicket stand of 87 - still the Welsh county's best for that wicket in one-day cricket - as Glamorgan ended on 155. By the time the Minor County openers took guard, the conditions were back in the batsman's favour, and despite a probing opening spell by both Nash and Cordle, Lincolnshire eased to a six-wicket victory with Maslin completing a fine game by completing an unbeaten 62.

29 June 1974 had not been a great day at Swansea for Glamorgan but not half as bad as 2 September 1927 turned out, quite literally, to be for Nottinghamshire after the East Midlands side arrived at the St. Helen's ground for their last match of the summer and on the cusp of winning the Championship title. In contrast, the Glamorgan players arrived at Swansea still seeking their first Championship win of the summer after 25 attempts. All that Nottinghamshire needed in order to clinch the county title was a draw against the Welsh county, and given their opponents' woeful form, plans had already been set in motion for a civic reception in Nottingham to celebrate their title-winning season.

All seemed to be going to plan as Nottinghamshire were dismissed for 233 after opting to bat first, before Eddie Bates and John Bell added 158 for the first wicket as the Glamorgan openers made an assertive reply. There were contributions as well from Arnold Dyson, Joe Hills and Dan Sullivan, as the home side amassed a first innings lead of 142 runs, but with only a day to go, and the wicket now appearing to be in a benign state, a draw still looked on the cards.

Jack Mercer then made inroads with the new ball as Nottinghamshire slipped to 23-2 before the close of play, but given the decent form of their batsmen, Lionel Kirk, the visiting captain had few worries as he dined with Trevor Arnott, his opposite number, in a hotel after play in Swansea besides fleshing out his speech for the next day's celebrations in Nottingham.

But the final morning proved to be a disaster for the visitors as the maritime and overhead conditions were in the bowlers favour. Jack Mercer exploited them to near perfection as he deceived 'Dodger' Whysall with a clever change of pace, causing the batsman to spoon a ball into the grateful hands of the fielder at short-leg. Soon afterwards, he bowled Wilfred Payton with an off-cutter, before yorking William Flint and bowling Lionel Kirk as he completed an eight-over spell with figures of 4/23.

At the other end, Ryan tricked and teased the visiting batsmen with his subtle spin, as seemingly every false stroke brought a wicket. The result was a steady procession of batsmen back to the Swansea pavilion, with each walking off in a state of disbelief, realising that their dream was turning

A view of the St. Helen's ground from the 1930s.

into a nightmare. Indeed, there is a tale that one of the Nottinghamshire tailenders sat outside the pavilion with tears flooding down his cheeks as his team-mates came back at regular intervals. Nottinghamshire were finally dismissed for 61 shortly before 12.15 pm, with Jack Mercer returning figures of 6/31 and later in the afternoon, Lancashire were declared county champions after what *Wisden* described as "the most sensational feature of the season" and over the year.

But the St. Helen's wickets have not just been a bowler's paradise, and there have been countless times over the years where a series of batsmen have prospered on the dry, sandy surface. In the words of Alan Jones, the legendary Glamorgan batsman and now Club President, "they have basically been decent batting wickets, thanks to the hard work of the groundstaff over the years, especially George Clements. Sometimes, the overhead elements have conspired against batsmen, but the bowlers have not always been on top."[2]

From a Glamorgan perspective, Alan is the best person to judge the quality of the wickets as 12 out of his 52 hundreds for the Welsh county came at St. Helen's - no batsman has been more prolific than the left-handed opener, with more recently Hugh Morris scoring eight, including two in a match against Nottinghamshire in 1993, whilst local boy Gilbert Parkhouse also scored eight out of his 32 first-class hundreds for Glamorgan on his home patch, including 121 against Leicestershire at St. Helen's on 7 May 1960 as he became the first and, so far, only Glamorgan batsmen to score a century against every county side.

Born in Swansea on 12 October, 1925, Gilbert Parkhouse learnt his cricket in the nets at Swansea under the watchful eye of Billy Bancroft before his skills were further honed at Wycliffe College in Gloucestershire. He had

Alan Jones seen during the late 1970s at Swansea with his son Andrew, who also played for Glamorgan in 1993.

first appeared in scratch county elevens during the wartime friendlies and National Service meant that Gilbert did not make his debut for Glamorgan until 1948. However, he swiftly made up for lost time by scoring over 1,000 runs in his debut season with his maiden Championship hundred also coming that summer, most appropriately at St. Helen's, against Sussex.

He went on to pass the thousand-run mark on another fourteen times consecutively until his career finished in 1962, by which time he had amassed a grand total of 23,508 first-class runs - a tally which still places him fourth in the all-time run scorers list for the Welsh county. But it was not just the weight of runs which Gilbert made, it was the way in which he made them, with contemporaries regarding Gilbert as the most elegant, yet destructive batsman of the post-war era. Indeed, Alan Jones, his opening partner in the early 1960s, is in no doubt about the air of cultivated annihilation which was associated with Gilbert's batting.

> "He was certainly the best Glamorgan opening batsman I have ever seen or played with. In my 25 years [as a player] I've opened with over twenty different players at Glamorgan, and apart from two imports, Majid and Javed, I would rate Parkhouse the best batsman I've player with for the county, with Tony Lewis a close second." [3]

Tony himself was fulsome of praise of Gilbert's efforts:

> "Gilbert was a very special player. He would take the ball late and run it off. I grew up as a kid watching him play in 1948 with his flowing drives. He was a class performer. The way he played [Frank] Tyson was beautiful because he could hook. Gilbert had amazing timing and footwork. He was one of those players who never slogged the ball... it just went. Colin Cowdrey used to get a large score at Canterbury and you never heard the ball on the bat all afternoon. Gilbert was similar. He was embryo top-class." [4]

Gilbert Parkhouse walks out to the middle at St. Helen's in 1952 with his long-serving opening partner Emrys Davies.

Out of the eight centuries and 22 fifties that Gilbert recorded in Championship cricket for Glamorgan at Swansea, perhaps the most remarkable, given the context on the game was his century which steered his side to victory against Worcestershire at St. Helen's during the middle of May 1959. Not only was it the Welsh county's first victory of the summer, it was made when several players, including Gilbert, were carrying injuries. A severe leg strain was enough to prevent Wilf Wooller from taking to the field so Allan Watkins was in charge.

Despite having strained the muscles in one leg and badly bruised the other, Gilbert felt fit enough the play and with his name in the Test selectors notebooks and calls for his recall to the England side, he did not want to miss out on any opportunities to add to his tally of England caps. But to make matters worse, Bernard Hedges, his opening partner, pulled a groin muscle on the first day's play so when the pair went out to chase a target of 263 on the final afternoon, Bernard had to have the help of a runner.

It was far from being the recipe for success but after hobbling around at first, Gilbert unleashed some typically elegant strokes, besides unfurling some textbook defensive strokes and, despite wincing pain, he occupied the crease for five and a half hour during which time he shared an opening stand of 170 with his infirm partner before ending up unbeaten on 111. No surprise that the following morning the *Western Mail* carried the headline 'Crocks Crack Way to Fine Win!'

Gilbert Parkhouse is congratulated on his England call-up in 1950 by Billy Bancroft, the former Glamorgan player who had first coached him as a youngster during the 1930s. Emrys Davies looks on approvingly.

A view of the St. Helen's ground from the Patti Pavilion in 1934.

Gilbert was also injured during Glamorgan's match against the 1956 Australians at St. Helen's. He was not alone on the physio's table as Jim Pressdee also took a blow and without a 13th man, an emergency announcement was made for another fielder. Sat in the crowd was the then seventeen year old Alan Jones who was on the junior staff. As he recalled:

> "Phil Thomas, the assistant secretary came over the tannoy and said 'Is there anybody in the ground from the Glamorgan staff? Could you report to the pavilion!' I heard that and went to the pavilion. They wanted me to go on and field but I had no kit with me. So they showed me Bernard Hedges' spare kit. We were the only two people in the club who were the same size! So I had his boots and all of his spare kit on as I walked down the steps and out onto the ground in front of so many people. When you were a kid, nothing meant more than wearing the daffodil and here I was for the first time in a big Glamorgan match wearing Bernard's kit! To cap it off, the first person to hit a ball to me on the field was Neil Harvey, my hero."[5]

1. T.Heald, *The Character of Cricket* (Pavilion Books, 1986).
2. A.Jones, with T.Stevens, *Hooked on Opening* (Gomer Publishing, 1984).
3. Ibid.
4. S.Hedges, *The Player from Ponty* (Welsh Academic Press, 2018).
5. op.cit.

Chapter Nine

"Good Old Johnnie"

Over the years, the St. Helen's ground has witnessed some remarkable and record-breaking feats by some unlikely batting partnerships. In 1981 the tenth wicket pair of all-rounder Rodney Ontong plus leg-spinner Robin Hobbs entered the Glamorgan record books by adding an unbeaten 140 for the tenth wicket during the County Championship match against Hampshire.

But the record created by the young South African and veteran Englishman was erased at Swansea the following year as reserve wicketkeeper Terry Davies together with Durham-born seam bowler Simon Daniels added 143 for the tenth wicket against Gloucestershire. The efforts of Davies and Daniels have still to be surpassed for the Welsh county, as do the efforts of another unlikely duo in Johnnie Clay and Joe Hills, who in 1929 added what still remains as a record 203 for the ninth wicket in Glamorgan's match against Worcestershire.

Whilst Johnnie Clay was a very familiar figure in Welsh sporting circles, his partner in the record stand at St. Helen's was less well-known. Born in Plumstead in Kent in 1897, Joe Hills had shown great promise as a schoolboy sportsman but on leaving school in 1915 he initially trained to be an electrician before enlisting with the Royal Engineers in mid-May 1916. The eighteen year-old then spent time at Hitchin Signals Depot before going to France on 7 January 1917 with the BT Cable Section. He soon saw active service on the Western Front, ensuring that cabling and other wiring from Brigade HQ reached the forward positions.

During the summer of 1918 he was involved in manoeuvres associated with the Hundred Days Offensive and on 27 August 1918, amidst heavy shelling and gunfire during the Battle of Amiens, he showed great bravery in ensuring that the communication links were maintained between Brigade HQ and the forward lines in what proved to be a decisive passage of warfare. His efforts did not go unnoticed and he duly received the Military Medal for his brave deeds.

He subsequently returned to civilian life in Kent and continued to show rich promise in both football and cricket, before securing a place on the Kent groundstaff, besides having trials as a goalkeeper with various Football League clubs. During the mid-1920s, he secured a professional contract with Cardiff City, and on New Year's Day 1925 he made his debut for the 'Bluebirds' against Sunderland.

Following his move to South Wales, he also secured a professional post with Barry CC, and his fluent strokeplay, classical cover drives and neat

Joe Hills.

wicketkeeping attracted the attention of Glamorgan's officials who were looking for a young and agile person behind the stumps. Terms were agreed for the 1926 season, and Joe soon proved to be a useful acquisition for Glamorgan, recording his maiden hundred against Nottinghamshire on a quite lively Trent Bridge wicket.

In 1926/27 Joe had a spell as goalkeeper with Swansea Town, before joining Fulham as their reserve goalkeeper, but in September, he broke his forearm and ruptured elbow ligaments in a reserve team game. Although he was able to return to action later in the season, he was increasingly handicapped by the injury, so he retired from football, and concentrated on cricket. The injury also meant that he gave up keeping wicket, and he played as a specialist batsman for the next few seasons.

As befitted someone who had been decorated for gallantry, Joe featured in several stubborn lower-order partnerships, adding 202 for the eighth wicket with Dai Davies against Sussex at Eastbourne in 1928, followed by the unbroken 203 with Johnnie Clay for the ninth wicket against Worcestershire in 1929 which gave the Swansea crowd one of those rare treats which are gloriously funny for home supporters. In just over an hour and a quarter, the pair had bludgeoned a stand worth 150 for the ninth wicket, with a series of withering drives and pulls to all parts of the St. Helen's ground.

During their stand, Clay frequently ran two or three yards down the pitch to drive Fred Root on the half volley. One straight drive cleared Mumbles Road and landed in the goods yard of the Swansea Bay station on the Mumbles Railway, bouncing and smashing through an office window. Hills also used a series of short-arm jabs plus firm punches off the back foot to further accumulate.

This was the heyday of Joe Hills' career with Glamorgan as in 1931 he was one of several professionals to be released at the end of the season as an economy measure. He later returned to the county circuit as an umpire and in 1947 stood in the Fourth Test of England's series against South Africa. Joe remained on the umpire's list until 1956, during which time he earned a reputation as a cheerful and popular official, and perhaps drawing on his grim experiences in the trenches, he was always ready to pass on a word of encouragement to a young player who was down on his luck. He retired from umpiring in 1956 after standing in 273 first-class matches. He subsequently died in Bournemouth on 21 September, 1969, just a few weeks after his former county had become county champions for the second time in their history.

There were other games during the 1930s when Johnnie Clay used the long handle with a variety of well-heeled amateurs at the other end, plucked from club cricket, and in the hope that they could make an impact at county level. One of these was Tony Duncan, better known as a golfer, who was invited to play for Glamorgan after taking part in century opening stands in the Rugby-Marlborough match at Lord's and making an undefeated century in a Freshman's match at Oxford University. Duncan duly played against Somerset at Swansea in 1934, and as he later recalled:

> "I made 15 not out in 75 minutes, holding up an end while Mercer and Clay hit sixes from the other end. We won the match despite a boisterous 92 by Arthur Wellard with a lot of sixes. I fielded in the deep when Wellard mis-hit. They luckily went over me for six. When he really got hold of them, they went clean out of the ground, over the Mumbles Road and onto the railway."[1]

Johnnie Clay also produced a string of outstanding bowling performances at Swansea during the 1930s and in 1937 he returned career-best figures in the Welsh county's match against Worcestershire as he took 9/66 in the first innings, followed by 8/146 in the second to finish with a Club record analysis of 17/212, and all on a shirt-front wicket which gave little assistance to the other slow bowlers in the game.

His masterclass in the art of off-spin came during a purple spell in mid-summer during which he also took nine for 59 against Essex at Westcliff, and prompted an approach from the Test selectors who wanted the genial off-spinner to ply his wares for King and Country against the 1938 Australians. He had already played for England in the Fifth Test of the series with the 1935 Springboks but, three years on, he was none too certain, largely as a result of various leg injuries.

Johnnie, as a fervent supporter of National Hunt racing, had bizarrely sustained one of these injuries whilst demonstrating to his family the prowess of the great steeplechaser Golden Miller in winning the Cheltenham Gold Cup. Unlike his equine hero, Clay tripped up whilst leaping over a series of obstacles placed on the lawn of his home. But the leg injury he sustained put great doubt on his ability to play cricket over three days or more and, as a result, he wrote to the England selectors,

Johnnie Clay leads out the Glamorgan side at Swansea in 1937 for their County Championship match against Sussex.

politely thanking them for their offer, but suggesting that instead they chose a younger and fitter man.

But 1937 did see a Glamorgan cricketer appear in Test cricket as Austin Matthews had an eventful return to the county circuit having parted ways with his previous employers Northamptonshire at the end of the 1936 season. His dramatic elevation into the England team followed a chain of events starting in early July when Jack Mercer suffered an injury to tendons in his left leg during the match against Lancashire at Blackpool. In his absence, George Lavis was pressed into service as an opening bowler, but he lacked the skill and guile of Jack, leaving the buoyant Glamorgan side bereft of an experienced medium-pacer.

By great fortune, Austin had met up with his old friend Maurice Turnbull after visiting his family in South Wales having completed a coaching stint at Stowe School. Austin and Maurice had played cricket and rugby together back in the mid-1920s before the Penarth-born sportsman moved to the East Midlands, to play rugby for Northampton and subsequently cricket for Northamptonshire. After hearing about Jack's ailments, Austin agreed to help out for the next few weeks. The MCC authorised his signing, and after making his Glamorgan debut against Gloucestershire at Newport he produced an outstanding spell against the New Zealanders, as described by the correspondent of the *Western Mail*:

> "He delivered an opening onslaught which was almost sensational in its devastating effects. With the second ball of his first over, Matthews uprooted Mooney's middle stump. In came big Tom Lowry but he was taken at the wicket off the next delivery and the crowd's roar was hushed - could he accomplish the hat-trick in the first over of an innings before a run had been scored? Turnbull closed in the field, but [Lindsay] Weir resisted the temptation to play at a good length ball pitched outside the off stump."[2]

Matthews went on to claim two further scalps as he ended with the fine figures of 4/49 as the tourists were dismissed for 127 with Emrys Davies claiming the last three wickets at a cost of just one run. With Glamorgan having a first innings lead of 102, Davies then put the Kiwis to the sword with the bat as he added 157 in the space of two hours and a quarter with his opening partner Arnold Dyson. Their run spree delighting the crowd, estimated at around 11,000 and described as by Nomad of the *Western Mail*: .

> "Hundreds were in their shirt sleeves and improvised paper hats and handkerchiefs of all colours of the rainbow were used as a protection against the scorching sun. Like Sydney Hill itself was the comment of one of the New Zealanders who told me that the Swansea crowd was the best they had seen at a county game this season."[3]

Maurice Turnbull declared the Glamorgan second innings around ninety minutes before the close on the second day, leaving the tourists with a target of 442. They had already lost three batsmen before the close and with a victory out of the question, many expected an attritional final day's play with the Kiwi's trying to save the game. To the glee of the locals, it only took Glamorgan forty minutes to wrap up victory with Johnnie Clay in vintage form, taking 5/27 as the Welsh county completed a comprehensive victory by 332 runs. The ease at which they won the game however did not take Nomad by surprise:

> "New Zealand were overawed by the gigantic task which faced them. Glamorgan's brilliant cricket the previous day had placed the tourists in a hopeless position, still 371 behind and with the ball turning on a worn wicket, they were a doomed side!"[4]

Whilst the plaudits on the final day rightfully went to Johnnie, tributes were paid to Austin's seam bowling and his new ball spell on the opening day which had literally put the tourists on the back foot. It turned out to be a purple patch for the experienced bowler as in the next Championship match against Sussex at Hastings, he took seven wickets in each innings. His career-best return of 14/132, on a perfect batting strip, set many tongues wagging, and not just in the Glamorgan camp either.

The England selector Percy Perrin had travelled to the south coast,

Austin Matthews.

ostensibly to watch Emrys Davies after his fine all-round performance against the Kiwis at Swansea, Although Emrys struck a sound hundred, it was Austin's hostile bowling that caught Perrin's eye. He duly followed up with a further six wickets against Somerset at Weston-super-Mare, and on 9 August – just thirteen days after his Glamorgan debut – the England selectors drafted him into their squad for the Third Test, in place of Freddie Brown.

The dramatic return of Austin Matthews to the county circuit in 1937 and the appearance of another Welshman in Test cricket may have brought a smile to Glamorgan's supporters, but their wafer-thin playing resources were cruelly exposed the following year as, on 1 July, they were beaten by the Swansea Central League in a time-limit evening match at St. Helen's. The game saw each side batting for an hour and a quarter but after the Swansea men made 121-7, the county side were restricted to 89-8 as the local cricketers celebrated a famous victory.

1. Bob Harragan pers.comm.
2. *Western Mail*, 2 August 1937.
3. *Western Mail*, 3 August 1937.
4. *Western Mail*, 4 August 1937.

Chapter Ten
Wartime and after

The victory over the New Zealanders was one of five at Swansea which Glamorgan recorded during 1937 as, for the first time in their history, the Welsh county won all of their first-class games at St. Helen's, with their outstanding form propelling Maurice Turnbull's team into seventh spot in the Championship table.

Their winning sequence began in the first week of May with an innings defeat of Kent. Arnold Dyson and Dai Davies each posted hundreds on the opening day before Closs Jones, the 25 year-old off-spinner, claimed 5/38 as the visitors were forced to follow-on. This was followed a month later by a 59-run victory over Hampshire before three weeks later the Clay-inspired win by nine wickets over Worcestershire, before the fourth Championship victory came during mid-July as Northamptonshire were beaten by 102 runs, thanks to a cultured century by Turnbull and a nine-wicket match haul by Clay.

After Glamorgan defeated Nottinghamshire by ten wickets in the first match of the 1939 season at St. Helen's during the first week of June, a few wags speculated that it might see a repeat of their unbeaten feat two years before. But draws duly followed against Hampshire and Leicestershire, before defeats during August against Surrey and the West Indians. By this time, though, people had other very pressing matters on their mind, but the exciting game with the tourists from the Caribbean gave them a chance to dwell on more pleasurable things.

Batting first, Glamorgan were dismissed for 127, with Learie Constantine taking 4/33 and leg-spinner Bertie Clarke 4/42, before Austin Matthews skittled the tourists for 96, taking 7/21 in what was his last hurrah on the county stage. Constantine was a handful again in the second innings, but some lusty blows by Haydn Davies during a forthright innings of 58 in the second innings saw Glamorgan to 159. The St. Helen's enclosures were full of excited chatter about another Welsh victory over the West Indians and a double over the tourists following their defeat at the Arms Park over the Whitsun Bank Holiday. But a dogged innings by Joe Stollmeyer guided the West Indians home with eight wickets down and with a day to spare.

Swansea enjoyed a decent summer in the South Wales and Monmouthshire League, with Reg Anderson, a fast-bowling policeman, spearheading their bowling whilst Percy Holmes, the former Yorkshire and England opening batman, bolstered their batting. The club appeared to be in rude health, but by late July, plans had been set in motion by Swansea Corporation for the ground to be used yet again by the military. Training camps were in operation by September as men in military uniforms replaced the regular

An aerial view of the St. Helen's ground.

occupants in their white shirts and flannels.

One concession brokered by the Corporation with the military authorities was for the cricket square, so beloved by the Bancrofts and the Crebers, to be roped off allowing some basic work being done on it by an interim groundsman. There had been talk of festival matches over the August Bank Holiday of 1940, to bolster both the coffers of the Club and to help lift morale, but the idea was abandoned as the Government called for factories to keep working and build up replacements for military equipment lost in the defeats and hasty retreat from northern France.

With Swansea badly blitzed by the Luftwaffe in 1941 it was some time before anyone had time to think again of cricket as entertainment. The local league went into hibernation after 1940, though many clubs and works sides kept up a programme of friendlies. Glamorgan organised a game at the Arms Park in 1942, and ran a series of matches in 1943, on the Barry Island, which, as in the Great War, staged matches to channel the energies of those employed in the busy port on the South Wales coast.

The rugby ground at St. Helen's also held a number of fund-raining rugby matches from 1942 onwards, as well as an American football match in December 1943. Each was well-attended with the Wales-England international on 7 March 1942 being watched by a crowd estimated at 20,000 raising over £1,900 for service charities. Over 15,000 were also present during March 1944 when a South Wales XV defeated a Dominions XV 42-19, whilst later in November, there were further bumper crowds at Swansea as firstly South Wales defeated NZ Services 32-14, whilst three weeks later Wales beat England 28-11.

By this time, cricket had returned to St. Helen's. First there was a time-limit match between a Glamorgan XI and the Swansea Central League, although few of the regular faces appeared in the county side. Bill Andrews of Somerset played, while Closs Jones made 35 and took 3/9, with Johnnie Clay also claiming 4/8. A one-day match followed in August against a National Fire Service XI. Willie Jones and local sportsman Harold Peters shared stand of 105 as Glamorgan declared at 203-7. Jones and Clay had another decent workout with the ball but the Fire Service held out for a draw, ending on 130-6.

With county games also taking place at Pontypridd, Barry and Newport, there had been discussions about another match at Swansea against the West of England, but the rough state of the outfield ruled this out, with the contest in mid-September being held instead at the Briton Ferry Steelworks club. Their efforts were reward the following summer with a one-day game in mid-June against Western Command, with Glamorgan securing a handsome 203-run victory after dismissing Western Command for just 68. With the remedial work having been completed on the turf at St. Helen's, two further matches were staged at Swansea.

The first took place on 21 July with a one-day contest against a Royal New Zealand Services XI who had secured a series of friendlies for their cricketing stars before heading home. It was captained by the Kiwi Test wicketkeeper Ken James, and included past and future internationals, including Stewie Dempster and Martin Donnelly. The match at Swansea was ruined by rain, with Glamorgan making 133-4 in what little play was

The young Gilbert Parkhouse being coached on the rugby ground at St. Helen's by Billy Bancroft during the 1930s.

possible, but there was sufficient time for young Gilbert Parkhouse to showcase his burgeoning talent with an impressive 71.

Gilbert was one of the bright young things of Glamorgan Cricket. Born in Swansea in October 1925, and educated both locally and at Wycliffe College in Gloucestershire, Gilbert had been coached from his earliest days at primary school by Billy Bancroft in the nets at St. Helen's. Jack Morgan takes up the story:

> "On his wanderings to St. Helen's as a boy in knickerbockers, Gilbert used to delight in taking a bat and they say even at that immature age he was natural little cricketer. He had been spotted by Billy Bancroft and a personal association between the veteran and the schoolboy grew up...
>
> Billy used to say that 'you cannot tell the youngsters a thing.' They knew it all or thought they did. But Gilbert was an eager pupil. At every opportunity Bancroft would be at the nets, showing the schoolboy the way it should be done, and so commenced Parkhouse's coaching - the first step in his initiation into the magic circle of cricket puritans, and which was to blossom so bountifully that he was selected to play for England at twenty-four years of age.
>
> Long before that they were saying at Swansea that Gilbert Parkhouse was a born cricketer and no-one had greater faith than Billy Bancroft."[1]

An image of Gilbert Parkhouse, Willie Jones and Wilf Wooller taken at Swansea in the early 1950s.

By the time county cricket resumed during 1946, Gilbert was on National Service and for a couple of years, at least, his first-class debut was put on hold. A full programme of county and club games were possible at St. Helen's that summer, but on several occasions, both the Swansea and Glamorgan elevens had an unfamiliar look about them with many of the pre-war stalwarts, like Gilbert, also on National Service. George Harris was still churning out the runs for Swansea in the South Wales and Monmouthshire League whilst the hearty efforts of Reg Anderson gave the policeman a chance to bowl with the new ball for Glamorgan against Hampshire.

With the County Championship having been re-instated, Northamptonshire were the first visitors to St. Helen's, although some of their bowlers must have wished they had stayed at home as the opening day of the contest saw Glamorgan rattle up 408-8. Thoughts of a Glamorgan victory though were literally washed out as it rained for the rest of the contest. Three weeks later Middlesex completed an innings victory at Swansea with Jim Sims claiming ten wickets in a match where the Glamorgan side included another policeman in Arthur Porter, then "Big-footed Arthur, they call me," the stalwart of the Newport club used to whimsically say, in parody of the wartime radio star 'big-hearted' Arthur Askey, who himself was an enthusiastic cricketer.

The first post-War victory for Glamorgan at Swansea duly came in July as Hampshire came west and were beaten by seven wickets. Emrys Davies made 119 on the first day, in a marathon effort taking ten minutes over four hours, and all whilst still on National Service and having to undertake guard duty at night in order to meet his military obligations. It certainly didn't affect his cricket too much as the all-rounder shared the bulk of the wickets with Johnnie Clay who spent the summer leading the county side and grooming it's next leader, Wilf Wooller.

A view from the Pavilion enclosures of Glamorgan's match against the 1946 Indians at St. Helen's.

The August Bank Holiday saw a game with the Indians and a huge crowd, in excess of 50,000 over the three days at Swansea. John Arlott was amongst them, with the fledgling broadcaster being part of the BBC commentary team who sent verbal reports to all parts of the Empire as well as penning quite brief, but typically eloquent ones for other media outlets. In this match, the man who became the doyen of post-war journalists wrote:

> "Some came early to get a seat then stood on it to see the play. The rugby grandstand was full up to a hundred yards from the boundary of the cricket field: uncounted dozens came in over the wall and hundreds turned from the closed gates to the seaside. All day the coupled electric tram-trains slid by the ground, giving a glimpse of the cricket gratis.
>
> When the loudspeakers called for Mr.Morris of Pontardawe to come and be twelfth man for the county team, every Welshman from Pontardawe, or nearby or who knew the said Mr.Morris, shouted his enthusiastic interest in county cricket. Mr.Morris presented himself - with modesty and enthusiasm but no gear - to be provided at once with clothing as prescribed for the playing of cricket and which, if it did not fit him with all the precision of a tailormade, would neither trip nor unduly confine him in the field.
>
> Glamorgan batted, seven Indians bowled and the same number of them dropped catches. E.L.James, comparatively new to county cricket, could not it seemed, believe his luck at being dropped by Test cricketers, so he hit up two more catches before he could be convinced - and remained not out - to ponder the kindness of fieldsmen." [2]

Thanks to this unbeaten 62 by Evan James, the locum from the Barry club, Glamorgan mustered 238. Vinoo Mankad claimed four wickets with his left-arm spin, but in the space of one remarkable over, Clay clubbed him for two straight sixes besides scything three fours. "The crowd cheered itself almost blue in the face," wrote Arlott.[3]

India replied with 203 thanks to 66 from Vijay Merchant with Clay also finding the conditions to his liking as he claimed 7/72 before Irishman Maurice Robinson top-scored with 72 in Glamorgan's second innings. The all-rounder had county experience with Warwickshire, as well as having appeared in wartime games in India whilst serving with the Royal Air Force. His appearances for the Welsh county stemmed from his posting to the St. Athan's camp in the Vale of Glamorgan, and though his forthright efforts, the Indians were set 273 in just over four hours.

This time the tourists went on the attack from the outset with Mushtaq Ali going for the bowling as in the space of an hour and a half he made 93 out of the Indian's total of 151. It gave them the launchpad they needed, and allowed others to play in a more sober fashion. But his efforts meant that the Indians were so far ahead of the clock that there was an hour to spare when the match was won by Ranga Sohoni hitting a pair of massive sixes off Clay.

But it was not all doom and gloom within Glamorgan's ranks as the well-attended game had boosted Glamorgan's accounts. £4,842 was taken on the gate, of which £934 went in entertainment tax and £1,766 to the Indians, whilst the scorecards brought in £121 5s 6d. It also heralded a return to normal in the calendar for the sports-lovers of Swansea and its environs, and mirroring the rebuilding work taking place in the town's bomb-damaged centre, the fact that Glamorgan, and their mix of old and new faces, were playing again on a regular basis at the ground overlooking Swansea Bay, provided an appetising mix of comfort and hope for those who had suffered the depravities of war both at home and on foreign fields.

It's business as usual at St. Helen's in 1946 as a large crowd watch the action in Glamorgan's Championship match against Leicestershire.

1. J.H. Morgan, *Glamorgan County Cricket* (Convoy Publications, 1952).
2. J.Arlott, *Indian Summer* (Longmans Green and Company, 1947).
3. ibid

Chapter Eleven

Championship tricks and a victory over the Boks

Wilf Wooller, the pre-war rugby international and amateur cricketer, had been amongst those to suffer at the hands of the Japanese whilst a Prisoner of War at various camps at Changhi. As sportsmen and women of the Swansea area dusted off their kit and got their equipment out of store, it seemed quite fitting that the burly all-rounder should be leading Glamorgan as the next chapter unfolded in the history of county cricket at St. Helen's with Wooller leading Glamorgan to the County Championship title in only his second year in charge.

It was Glamorgan's first-ever title with Wooller's team surprising what seemed like everyone outside Wales in winning the County Championship. Despite a few headshakes in the Home Counties following their decisive victory against Hampshire at Bournemouth in late August, it was not a fluke in 1948 and owed much to the strategy of Wooller, and the skills of his bowlers and fielders, with the latter forming a predatory ring close to the bat and building - in the case of Swansea - on the ground's reputation as a place which helped the spinners.

Wilf Wooller makes his way down the pavilion steps at Swansea with John Reid, the captain of the 1958 New Zealanders.

With confidence high, the spinners in fine form, and Wooller - like a British bulldog, snarling instructions plus a few insults from his position at short-leg - it is not surprising that, as in 1937 when they had risen up the table under the more genteel leadership of Maurice Turnbull, Wooller's men won four out of four Championship matches at St. Helen's during that daffodil golden summer of 1948.

Three of those games were dominated by the left-arm spin of Stan Trick, one of the stars of League cricket in West Wales during the years either side of the Second World War. Born in Briton Ferry in October 1916, Stan had shone at sport whilst at Cwrt Sart School and won a string of Welsh schools football caps. But, it was in cricket that he later hit the headlines, playing initially with honour for Briton Ferry Steel CC before leaving the employ of the local steelworks and working in his family's garage in Neath.

Stan Trick.

His duties in the business meant that Stan could rarely take time off to play in county cricket in the late 1930s. After the war, he remained one of the finest spin bowlers in the South Wales and Monmouthshire League and was a potent force with the ball whenever Neath played at St. Helen's. Johnnie Clay was acutely aware that Trick could be the trump card in Wooller's pack and after a few quiet words from the pair, Trick made himself available for all four Championship at Swansea, as well as the match against Warwickshire on his home patch at The Gnoll as Neath played host to the West Midlands side. In all, Trick took 28 wickets in the four matches at St. Helens and played a leading hand in victories which maintained Glamorgan's quest of the county title.

In late May Somerset were the first visitors to Swansea with Glamorgan in rude health after victories in three of their opening four matches. On a typically slow and dry surface, Glamorgan steadily accumulated 257 on the first day, with Phil Clift making a sedate half-century before some later blows by Wooller and Haydn Davies.

Somerset kept up with them, ending just eight behind, with Harold Gimblett rolling back the years with an elegant 70 before Arthur Wellard clubbed a few lusty blows of his own and for a short while put in peril the trains running along the railway line on the far side of the Oystermouth Road. Despite his salvo, Trick held his nerve and claimed 6/77 in his 34 overs. Nomad duly wrote in the *Western Mail*, "Trick impressed with his clever spin and would have returned better figures but for his meeting with the big-hitting Wellard."[1]

Emrys Davies and Gilbert Parkhouse then completed assured half centuries as Somerset were left with a target of 236. It proved to be too much as, with the wicket well worn, Trick was in his element, taking 6/29 to spin Glamorgan to another victory. Under the heading "Stan's six wickets did the Trick!", Nomad was fulsome once again in his praise of the spinner, noting his accuracy and variations, especially a sharp top-spinner:

> "Trick maintained an excellent length and great accuracy. Making the occasional ball rise sharply, Trick hit the wickets of five of his six victims and he promises to be of valuable assistance when available."[2]

His match-winning efforts with the ball saw Glamorgan rise into second place in the table and they consolidated their position with two further wins before Kent were the next visitors at St. Helen's. Once again, it was a bowler-friendly surface, with a few wags suggesting that the groundsman's preparations for the pitch had been focussed more on buckets of sand than using rollers or lawnmowers!

Twenty wickets fell on the first day with Phil Clift scoring 73 as Glamorgan reached 189 before Stan claimed 6/39 as Kent were spun out after tea for a paltry 105. On the second day, two left-handers completely changed the pattern of the match with Emrys Davies scoring 92 and Allan Watkins 93. After Wooller had declared, Kent were left with a mammoth 399 to win, but they mustered a mere 120 with Len Muncer claiming 5/47, whilst Stan played a fine supporting role and ended with 4/32 as the visitors capitulated, with Nomad writing "on a wicket taking spin, Kent never showed any fight as Glamorgan's bowlers demonstrated why they are second place in the Championship table."[3]

Muncer and Trick played a leading role a week later as Glamorgan defeated Nottinghamshire by 221 runs at St. Helen's with the game following a similar pattern with a top-order batsman wearing down the visiting attack, in this case Willie Jones who made a gritty 62, before some late blows from Wooller, who made 80 from number eight to see Glamorgan to 329. After securing a first innings lead of 112, Glamorgan's batsmen played with freedom and gleefully extended the lead with Emrys Davies making a forthright 75 to leave the visitors with a target of 300. They could only make 78 as Muncer came into his own, taking six wickets in his 19 overs which cost only 13 runs. Runs literally dried up as Trick was equally frugal

Stan Trick is on the far right of this image, taken at St. Helen's in 1948, as Wilf Wooller leads the Glamorgan side into the field.

at the other end, taking 2/24 as Glamorgan clinched another victory to maintain their place in the Championship table.

These victories had seen Glamorgan bat first, but the class of '48 showed that they could also win by bowling first on Swansea soil. This duly happened in early July as Sussex were beaten by six wickets, although such a scenario had seemed unlikely as John Langridge occupied the crease for just under four hours to compile a painstaking hundred. His opening partner Harry Parks made a half-century but once they were parted, Muncer then ran through the rest of the side to claim 8/99, with Trick again being the perfect foil at the other end delivering 45 accurate overs for just 64 runs. Sussex's final total of 261 was quite disappointing given Langridge's efforts and the home batsmen played with confidence and class on the wearing surface with Parkhouse scoring a brilliant maiden first-class hundred, as described below by Nomad:

> "The innings played by Parkhouse was a delight to watch because of the abundance of the all-around-the-wicket strokes which he employed. He was never over venturesome and he never crossed the border to recklessness. His hitting was generally crisp: it was never indecisive. The fluency of his strokeplay showed without a doubt that he is destined to get many hundreds."[4]

With Jim Eaglestone, Glamorgan's recent acquisition from Middlesex making 72 in 50 minutes, Glamorgan ended on 402 before Muncer and Trick got to work again as the pair of spinners exploiting the dry surface. The former ended with 7/102 from 45 teasing overs as Glamorgan were left with a modest target of 93 to win, and with confidence sky high in the home camp, they eased to a four-wicket win, with the strains of the

Welsh National Anthem once again emanating from the pavilion as the Glamorgan team celebrated another decisive victory.

These renditions of *Mae Hen Wlad fy'n Haddau* were easy for the Welsh-speaking contingent in Wooller's side, but as John Arlott recalled, they were less straightforward for the imports:

> "They had imported three former Middlesex players in Len Muncer, Jim Eaglestone and Norman Hever. The team habitually used to sing 'Land of My Fathers' in Welsh, which Hever, Muncer and Eaglestone strove to learn. Jim Eaglestone never made it. The other two did. I think they were the two who sang out of tune."[5]

Many of the spectators in and around the pavilion and member's enclosure joined in with these renditions, and with the 1948 Australians the next visitors to Swansea, there was much speculation about how Wooller and his title-seeking team would fare against Don Bradman's team who were enjoying unprecedented success on the 34-match tour and were well on the way to a 4-0 series win in the Test Matches.

Their presence at Swansea for the three-day game drew a club record aggregate of 50,000, and on the opening day, around 20,000 people were shoehorned into the ground. To the delight of the locals, Emrys Davies and Phil Clift shared a vibrant opening stand with the latter, impressing with some fluent strokes. They were parted after adding 53, and the Australians then made steady inroads into the home batting, despite a spritely cameo from Willie Jones, before Glamorgan were dismissed for 197.

The crowd at Swansea enjoying watching the match against the 1948 Australians.

Bill Brown and Sid Barnes began the Australian reply, but their line-up did not include Don Bradman, who had decided to sit out the match at Swansea in 1948. Local legend has it that on arriving in Swansea, the great 'Don' was eager to know the composition of the Glamorgan side, and whether or not Johnnie Clay was in the line-up. The silver-haired spinner was, and like Charlie Parker of Gloucestershire, his bowling prowess had left an indelible mark on Bradman's memory, so much so, that he decided to hand over the reins to Lindsay Hassett and watch from the sidelines.

The prospect of watching the Australians bat all day was still sufficiently attractive for a bumper crowd of 30,000 to descend upon Swansea the following morning, causing the gates to be closed before lunch was taken. Those fortunate enough to get into ground in the morning were treated to an aggressive innings of 84 from Keith Miller, who struck five sixes and seven fours before being well caught in the covers by Eaglestone after Clay had deceived the great Australian all-rounder into mis-timing another booming drive. But soon after Miller had made his way back to the pavilion, light rain started to fall. It soon intensified and forced the players off the field at 3pm. Sadly, they were never to return, as steady rain fell throughout the following day and the match was abandoned as a soggy draw.

A view of the packed rugby field at St. Helen's during Glamorgan's game against the 1948 Australians.

Despite the result, the atmosphere at St. Helen's had been intoxicating and many of the youngsters who caught the cricket bug became devotees of the Welsh county in succeeding years. The *hwyl* and passion filtered up to the press area, on the roof of the Swansea pavilion and as Jack Morgan, the leading sports journalist in South Wales and *Wisden's* correspondent for many years, duly wrote:

> "For me it is the ideal place to watch cricket, sitting between the pagodas at the top of the imposing pavilion, with one eye on the Bay and the other on the beautiful green oval below. The trains travelling to and fro into Swansea (Victoria) on the old L.M.S. line, and the electric trams chugging away with their loads of holiday makers to Mumbles, interrupt the gentle lapping of the waves. The wicket, too, gets better year by year and from the most senior County member down to the youngest 'boy' guzzlng' his bottle of 'pop' at the boundary's edge, there is shown a wonderful sense of loyalty towards the County."[6]

It was therefore with a great sense of Celtic pride that Wooller and his team played at Swansea in the coming years as many visiting teams strove to make amends for the county title having left England. But as Wooller was quite prepared to tell anyone eyeball to eyeball, Glamorgan's success in 1948 was not down to luck, and with some alert fielding and accurate bowling, especially on leg stump, the Welsh county had deservedly lifted the Championship title.

They also had some bright young talent, with Allan Watkins, becoming the first Glamorgan cricketer to score a Test Match century during the tour of South Africa in 1948/49, whilst Gilbert Parkhouse, was called up by the England selectors in 1950. After their success in 1948, Wooller's team ended in eighth place in 1949, and then eleventh spot in 1950 before bouncing back up into fifth place in 1951 – a summer which also saw them record one of the most remarkable victories in their history at Swansea as they became the only county side to defeat the 1951 South Africans, yet even the most partisan of Welshmen would have been hard pressed to forecast a Glamorgan win when Wooller's side were dismissed for a modest 111 after being put in on a rain-affected wicket.

The day had also begun poorly for Jim Pleass, a rookie professional from Cardiff during the Championship-winning season in 1948, but three year later now an established member of the Glamorgan line-up. As the batsman later recalled:

> "Huge traffic jams on the A48 to Swansea delayed my journey from Cardiff, and I arrived at the St Helen's ground just ten minutes before the scheduled start to find that Glamorgan had won the toss, and I was batting at number three. Really, I didn't have time to get my breath. Thirteen runs on the board, and our first wicket went down. The massive crowd did not bother me, but the swing bowlers did, and I soon edged a slip catch to Van Ryneveld, having scored just a single."[7]

Things improved for Jim and the rest of the Glamorgan side during the afternoon session, as once again Muncer exploited the St. Helen's wicket, taking 5/99 in a fine spell of off-spin, leaving the Springboks teetering at 34-7 at tea. After the interval Athol Rowan and Percy Mansell counter-attacked the bowling, adding 52 in even time for the eighth wicket, before the tourists were also dismissed for 111 to leave honours all square on first innings.

The following day was a Sunday and whilst the tourists spent time on the Gower Peninsula, the Glamorgan players spent a day at home before heading back to Swansea on the Monday. This time Pleass ensured that he allowed plenty of time for his journey, as he later remembered:

> "The Bank Holiday atmosphere at St Helen's was electric, Twenty-four thousand people had crammed into the ground; the weather was fine, and the wicket looked like a ploughed field. Glamorgan started their second innings, and as number three I was at the wicket once again within minutes, with Phil Clift having departed with only three runs on the board."[8]

With the St. Helen's wicket starting to take spin, Glamorgan's batsmen knew that they had to be positive in their approach. For his part, Wooller needed few invitations to attack the bowling, and if there was anyone who was not going to go down without a fight it was the Welsh county's leader. He hit a typically aggressive 46, and together with doughty support from Pleass, Glamorgan were able to set the tourists a target of 147.

Wilf Wooller and Jim Pleass make their long way down the pavilion steps as the pair go out to bat against the1951 South Africans at Swansea.

By tea on the second day, the South Africans had reached 54 without loss and the game appeared to be heading away from Glamorgan, as neither of their spinners seemed able to pierce the defence of Springbok openers John Waite or Russell Endean. During the interval, Wooller spoke to his team in the dressing room, cajoling them for one last effort, and telling them that all that was needed was one wicket, as others would quickly follow.

His words proved prophetic as a quite remarkable passage of play then followed, witnessed by an increasingly animated crowd of 25,000, as all ten wickets fell within the space of three quarters of hour, and all for just 29 runs. The chief tormentors were Muncer, who claimed 4/10, and Jim McConnon, who took 6/10, including a hat-trick. Both were aided by some breathtaking catches close to the wicket, including one by Wooller at silly mid-on, after deflecting a firm on-drive from Clive van Ryneveld and then clutching onto the rebound inches from the turf. Even Parkhouse, fielding as substitute for Emrys Davies, took two fine catches, and all despite nursing a wrist injury.

Believing to be in a winning position at tea, the bottom half of the South African batting order changed into their civvies thinking that they would not be needed out in the middle. It led to some strange sights, as Don Shepherd remembered as Michael Melle, the Springboks' fast bowler walked out to bat having been promoted up the order in a bid to hit the tourists out of trouble:

Jim McConnon.

> "He had already showered and changed, ready to go on the bus, but he had to come in before he had had time to change properly. He came out to the middle without his socks on, just a pair of boots, and that was that."[9]

Jim Pleass also remembered how the tourists were taken by surprise, and the joyous celebrations after the Glamorgan victory:

> "With the mad scramble to change back into whites and don pads, their dressing room must have looked like the opening day of a quick-change artistes' convention. But the wickets kept tumbling - 72-8 and 72-9 before Percy Mansell was caught by Gilbert Parkhouse off a top edge, and it was all over. We had won by 64 runs. Then the euphoria; we were mobbed and Wilf was carried shoulder-high from the field; the National Anthem was sung in the Pavilion and the champagne flowed yet again at St. Helen's."[10]

Jim Pleass late cuts Percy Mansell during his decisive innings with Wilf Wooller against the 1951 Springboks at Swansea.

1. *Western Mail*, 25 May 1948.
2. *Western Mail*, 26 May 1948.
3. *Western Mail*, 16 June 1948.
4. *Western Mail*, 9 July 1948.
5. J.Arlott, *Indian Summer* (Longman's Green and Company, 1947)
6. Article by J.H.Morgan, *"The County's Grounds"* in the Glamorgan CCC Yearbook for 1951.
7. A.K.Hignell, *Lucky Jim - The memoirs of Glamorgan's 1948 Championship winner* (Welsh Academic Press, 2014).
8. Ibid.
9. D.Miller, *Born to Bowl, Douglas Miller* (Fairfield Books, 2004).
10. A.K.Hignell op. cit.

Chapter Twelve

The Prince of Port Eynon

With over 2,000 first-class wickets to his name, Don Shepherd followed in a long line of off-spin bowlers from Harry Creber, through Len Muncer and, in more recent times, Robert Croft to prosper on the sandy-based surface at Swansea. Born and raised at Port Eynon on the Gower Peninsula, St. Helen's was Don's home ground from his debut season in 1950 until hanging up his bowling boots at the end of the 1972 season. It was also where his family held his wake following his death in August 2017, just a week or so after celebrating his 90th birthday.

In all, Shep played in 125 first-class matches at Swansea, delivering 26,244 balls and claiming 464 wickets at a fraction over 20 runs apiece. These achievements are set against his record of 371 wickets at the Arms Park, plus a further 96 from 1967 onwards at Sophia Gardens, taking his Cardiff tally to a mere three more than his Swansea one.

Shep's debut in Glamorgan's ranks at St. Helen's came on 17 June, 1950 during their County Championship match against Surrey with the 22 year-old run out for a single in his first innings at the ground which was to play such a major part of his life as a professional cricketer. Remarkably, Shep had rarely been to the ground before and even after his family had moved

Don Shepherd, pictured in 1950.

closer to Swansea during the mid-1930s to run the shop at Parkmill, he had never travelled to watch county cricket in Swansea. Apart from a few games at Gowerton County School for Boys, he had little experience of formal games and had spent most of his youth playing knockabout games with friends or watching the Port Eynon side with his grandfather, who was their scorer.

His rise into professional cricket had followed his National Service firstly with the Navy and then the Fleet Air Arm in the West Midlands with Don's abilities as a tearaway fast bowler whilst playing for RAF Defford attracting the attention of Worcestershire. A place on the MCC groundstaff for 1948 and a contract with the West Midlands club then followed, but after the intervention of Wilf Wooller and coach George Lavis, Shep went to Lord's as a Glamorgan cricketer.

He subsequently made his Glamorgan debut in 1950 and met with much success as a seam bowler, taking 120 wickets in 1952 before two years later claiming career-best figures of 9/47 against Northamptonshire at the Arms Park. The Cardiff ground became the venue for the first five of his 'ten-fors' on Welsh soil, and it was not until 1957, having converted during the previous summer to off-cutters, that Shep took his first ten-wicket haul at Swansea, returning figures of 6/20 and 4/71 in the match against Somerset. In all, he claimed 28 'ten-fors' during his long and illustrious career, with his Swansea returns including 10/107 against Kent in 1958, 10/134 against the 1959 Indians, and 11/54 against Warwickshire in 1960,

An image of the St. Helen's ground during the early 1950s.

before a last hurrah on his old stamping ground by returning figures of 6/33 and 6/106 against Derbyshire in 1970.

There are so many instances of Shep being the bane of visiting batsmen who were bamboozled by his subtle wiles on the dry, sandy surface at Swansea, with his finest hour with the ball at St. Helen's coming against Yorkshire during June 1965, as Glamorgan recorded a 31-run victory inside two days. It was also a game which saw Shep and his spin partner Jim Pressdee, each taking nine wickets in an innings – the only time in a first-class match where a pair of bowlers have each achieved this feat. Their remarkable performance saw Pressdee claim nine wickets in the visitors first innings before Shep opened the bowling and took nine in their second innings in a game where the highest individual score was 46 made by Doug Padgett.

Aware of the way that the St. Helen's wicket would assist the spin bowlers, captain Ossie Wheatley opted to bat after winning the toss, but only Alan Rees and Euros Lewis looked comfortable against the spin of Brian Close and Ray Illingworth. It was a great credit to the two Welshmen that Glamorgan made 140, as the Yorkshire batsmen were soon in deep trouble against the left-arm spin of Pressdee, who had returned to the side after missing a couple of matches with a leg strain.

Three batsmen got into the twenties, but nobody, not even the mighty Geoff Boycott, stayed for any lengthy period. The brilliant run out of Jack Hampshire by Peter Walker at short-leg halted the procession against Pressdee's bowling, and stopped him from emulating Jack Mercer's feat of taking ten wickets in an innings, achieved at Worcester in 1936. Even so, Pressdee quickly mopped up the tail, and ended with career-best figures of 9/43 as Glamorgan gained a valuable first innings lead of 44 runs. Although Shep had claimed no wickets, he had bowled quite brilliantly at the other end and as JBG Thomas wrote

> "Pressdee tried to make Shepherd lead the team up the pavilion steps. But Shepherd refused and pushed Pressdee ahead of him, through the clapping crowd which stood to thunder their applause for a memorable achievement."[1]

When Glamorgan batted for a second time, Yorkshire opened the attack with their spinners rather than calling upon the services of fiery pace bowler Fred Trueman. It proved to be a shrewd move as Ray Illingworth and Don Wilson made short work of the Welsh county's second innings. For the second time in the game, Euros Lewis offered doughty resistance, but wickets tumbled at the other end, as Glamorgan slumped to 93-9.Some 'old fashioned' tail end hitting by Shep and Ossie Wheatley then tipped the balance back in Glamorgan's favour, as the pair added 28 invaluable runs to set up an intriguing finale.

Yorkshire needed 166 to win and they lost an early wicket as Don took the new ball and swiftly dismissed Ken Taylor. But Boycott and Padgett steadied the ship and shared a productive second wicket stand of 64 to regain the initiative for the Tykes, until Boycott was superbly caught by Walker off Pressdee's bowling. His departure heralded a remarkable collapse against Shepherd's off-cutters, but Pressdee had a funny feeling that it would be Shep's day: "After Don had taken the first wicket, I had a feeling it was going to be his turn. I hoped he would do as well as I had in the first innings."[2]

Only Jack Hampshire, with two mighty sixes and five fours, offered anything more than token resistance against Shepherd's clever bowling. The wily bowler took the final eight wickets in fairly quick succession, to finish off with figures of 9/48 as Glamorgan completed another remarkable victory at St. Helen's. His feat was witnessed by Johnnie Clay, who was the Club's President and the man, who had achieved the feat on three occasions during his illustrious career, was very pleased to witness the efforts of a fellow member of the spinners' union.

But as JBG Thomas wrote in the *Western Mail*, Johnnie witnessed Shep's feat:

> "whilst perched uncomfortably on a stone wall on the roof of the pavilion all through the innings, and told others that he was sitting there when the first innings fell and that he would not be moving until the last one goes down. Whilst Johnnie remained on his perch, Shep steadily worked his way through the Yorkshire batting, shouting appeals for lbw and having some fine catches taken close to the wicket as the ball spat.
>
> Don Wilson then showed every intention of cracking the ball out of the ground and with almost the entire Glamorgan team in deep catching positions, Shep lured him down the pitch. David Evans made no mistake in whipping off the bails to give the off-cutter his ninth and final wicket. Shepherd's arms were soon in the air and Johnnie slid off his perch, smiling the secret smile of the cricketer who knows that superstition really counts in this game."[3]

It was a bitter-sweet time however for Shep, because few at the ground, or even colleagues in the Glamorgan changing room, were aware that he had achieved this remarkable feat having had virtually no sleep the night before. Instead, he had sat up at his ailing father-in-law's bedside and later that day heard the sad news that his wife's father had passed away.

Four years before the Swansea ground saw Shep play one of his most remarkable innings; in fact, to many of the Glamorgan faithful present at St. Helen's that day, it was one of the most remarkable they had seen anyone play. It came during Glamorgan's match against the 1961 Australians, and is considered now by the game's historians as helping to set the tone for a decade when Glamorgan defeated the men in baggy green caps on successive tours and clinched another Championship title.

To the delight of a packed St. Helen's, Shep equalled the world record for the fastest fifty in first-class cricket, racing to his half-century in just fifteen minutes, with eleven scoring strokes, and all whilst sporting a black eye having top-edged a ball trying to sweep Gloucestershire's David Allen into his eye in the previous match at Pontypridd. In fact, the blow had sent him tumbling to the grass at Ynysangharad Park where he lay for a few seconds in a semi-conscious state.

In today's game, there are protocols in place where players have to miss games on medical grounds, but it was a very different world back in 1961 and with the help of a few aspirins, Shep took his place in the team for the next match at Swansea, despite having his eye still half-shut. He did not want to let the team down as they tried to do better than in the earlier game that summer against the tourists over the Whitsun Bank Holiday at the Arms Park. It had been a game when Glamorgan should have followed-on had Bobby Simpson and others not needed batting practice.

It had been a good game though for Pressdee who struck 118 and became Glamorgan's first centurion against Australia on Welsh soil, whilst Parkhouse made a fine 70. Unfortunately, Parkhouse was injured for the Swansea match and was replaced by the next batting icon from the west, left-hander Alan Jones. While Alan may have been born only a short distance from the Swansea ground, his home village of Velindre is much more rural and there has always been the feel of the countryman about Alan. That rubbed off on his batting, particularly in his unruffled ability to bat all day. Not that he had a chance this early in his career as Ron Gaunt had him lbw for a duck.

The Australians had batted first, although there were a few grumbles about the conditions and a bit of dampness in the wicket. With people thronging in and plenty of blue sky overhead, it would have been poor PR had there been a lengthy delay, so the tourists made a steady and watchful start against the seam bowling of Clydach's Brian Evans and the Welsh county's new skipper, Ossie Wheatley – or "Dai Peroxide" as the former Warwickshire and Cambridge University bowler had been christened. The introduction of Shep's off-cutters, saw Simpson depart for 23, but Bill Lawry and Norm O'Neill settled in to each score sixties, before both departed to Walker. A collapse then followed as none of the other batsmen reached double figures with Don finishing with figures of 5/50 as, in the words of JBG Thomas:

> "The true Test Match atmosphere took possession of the historic St. Helen's ground... with the immaculate off-spin of Don Shepherd and the tireless support of Peter Walker. The dream which perhaps one day will produce an Australian Test Match at Swansea is well worthwhile and Saturday's play contained all the seeds of such a future event."[4]

The glee on the faces of the Glamorgan supporters at seeing the tourists dismissed for 192 soon disappeared on the second day as the Australians, suitably galvanized by excursions on the Gower during Sunday, swiftly reduced the Welsh county to 94-8 with the architects of their sharp, and quite sudden, decline being leg-spinner Richie Benaud and slow left-armer Lindsay Kline, who each found plenty of assistance from the now quite dry and dusty wicket. The clatter of wickets shocked the crowd into silence, but down the long flight of steps at the Swansea ground came the unlikely

Don Shepherd pictured whilst he was batting with Tom Graveney at the Scarborough Festival.

saviour of Glamorgan's fortunes in the shape of Donald John Shepherd.

In the blink of an eye 'Shep' was soon into double figures as the ball sped to, and over, the boundary ropes as the Glamorgan tail-ender unleashed some furious blows. With his partner David Evans reduced to a watching brief at the other end, 'Shep' raced to his fifty with six massive sixes, three each off each spinner, plus three other fours, a quickly scampered two and a hastily run single - to equal the world record, and to prompt a euphoric report by JBG Thomas in the following morning's *Western Mail*:

> "Whether Glamorgan lose or save this exciting match today, it will be known and remembered at least in Wales as Shepherd's match. Every big hit was cheered and it set the tempo for the day as well as putting Glamorgan back into proceedings and ensuring a third day's play. We wondered whether Glamorgan would reach the 100-mark as Shepherd walked to the wicket. Little did we realise what was in store for us, but it came as an even greater surprise to the lively Australians. Crash, bang, wallop went Shepherd with well-timed rustic swings. His efforts could not have been better timed. The Australians enjoyed it too, and readily applauded some remarkably big hits."[5]

His rousing efforts lifted the spirits of the home supporters, and the Glamorgan team alike, with Glamorgan ending just 43 runs in arrears.

Despite a fine century from Bobby Simpson, the Welsh batsmen were able to save the game, as a downpour washed out play with just over two hours to play and with the tourists still needing eight wickets. Glamorgan's spirited fightback, inspired by Shep's feat, had been a moral victory for the home side as the Australians left the damp and deserted Swansea ground thinking what might have been, had it not been for his remarkable innings.

As the consummate team man and senior professional, Shep was never one to boast about his personal achievements. "I just had a bit of luck and a good old swing with the bat that day," he would modestly say when asked about events that August afternoon. Whereas other players take great delight in recalling blow by blow as they brag about their finest innings, Shep would just unashamedly smile and with a glint in his eye, the only additional sign about how he felt about his personal achievement and a place in the record books.

But his whirlwind fifty had not been in a winning cause, and Shep's two proudest days in Glamorgan's ranks at Swansea were undoubtedly when he led the county to victory over the 1968 Australians, and the following August when Glamorgan completed a dramatic one-run victory over Essex to leave them within one victory of clinching the 1969 Championship title.

Don Shepherd (left) congratulates Robert Croft after the all-rounder had taken his 1,000th first-class wicket for Glamorgan at Swansea in 2011.

1. *Western Mail*, 10 June 1965.
2. D.Miller, *Born to Bowl* (Fairfield Books, 2004).
3. *Western Mail*, 11 June 1965
4. *Western Mail*, 7 August, 1961
5. *Western Mail*, 8 August 1961

Chapter Thirteen
The Extra Test Match

The early twentieth century saw St. Helen's acquire the feel of a sporting amphitheatre. In 1923, the imposing wooden grandstand was erected adjacent to the Mumbles Road, whilst the raised banking – initially made of turf – was added in the late 1920s, followed by the creation of the elevated bank at the eastern end of the ground. As a result, it was an intimidating venue, especially when the chants or cheers echoed around the ground during the Welsh rugby internationals, staged at the Swansea ground on a regular basis until 10 April 1954 when Wales defeated Scotland 15-3.[1]

It was here, during the following decade, in the summer theatre of Welsh sporting dreams that Glamorgan achieved stunning victories on back-to-back tours by the Australians. This was a period when Glamorgan's grounds at Swansea and Cardiff hosted matches against the tourists over the Whitsun and August Bank Holidays. Watched by enormous crowds, all wanting the Welsh county to beat the touring teams, these matches at St. Helen's soon earned the nickname of being the 'Extra Test Match.'

Don Shepherd recalled the excitement and the massive crowds at these matches:

> "I can remember 32,000 in there on an August Bank Holiday Monday against one of the Australian touring sides. I always felt that there was something special about the tourist matches. People had come to enjoy them, and there was applause for a good stop in the field or a good throw, not just clapping for a hundred or five wickets. It's nice to know that your efforts are appreciated all the way along the line, and in the matches against the tourists, everything seemed a bit extra special to the crowd."[2]

Those present in 1964 were able to share in a very special piece of Glamorgan's history as they beat for the first-ever time the men in baggy green caps. When Bobby Simpson and his fellow Australians arrived in the UK, only one county – Surrey – could claim to have beaten an Australian touring team since 1912. In this time, some of the greatest names in English cricket had pitted their skills against the Australians, and only the mighty Surrey side of the 1950s had come out on top.

By the time Simpson and his men got to Swansea, they had maintained their unbeaten record in the county games, whilst they were already one-up in the Test series. With Glamorgan enjoying a modest season – having just three wins to their name from twenty Championship matches – it looked odds-on that the Australians would maintain this unbeaten sequence.

But, as they say, records are there to be broken and during the course

The victorious Glamorgan team, led by Ossie Wheatley, which defeated the 1964 Australians at Swansea.

of the next few days, Glamorgan turned the formbook upside down, and all with a quite inexperienced side, as captain Ossie Wheatley opted to rest several senior players. Few in the crowd of around 20,000 must have fancied a Glamorgan win as the Welsh county were bundled out for 197, but after a short shower had freshened up the Swansea wicket, Shepherd and Pressdee produced a magnificent spell of bowling as Australia slumped to 39-6 with the cream of their batting talent sent packing by Glamorgan's spin-twins.

It wasn't just the fans in the St. Helen's ground who were willing on the Glamorgan team as the National Eisteddfod was being held just a mile or so down the road from the Swansea ground. The organisers had shown great enterprise in arranging for television screens to be placed around the tented village, and the sets drew an ever-increasing crowd as word spread around the *maes* of Glamorgan's fightback, resulting in hundreds of patriotic Welshmen and women eager to catch a glimpse of the flickering black and white images, courtesy of the coverage provided by BBC Wales. The two teams also made an appearance on stage, as remembered by Alan Jones:

> "as both teams took to the stage that night at the Royal National Eisteddfod in Swansea, who would have known we were just a few days away from an historic victory."

Shep also remembers that night and suggests that, "after going up on the stage, we were so full of *hwyl* that there was no way we were going to lose that match." The following morning, Glamorgan's bowlers polished off

Australia for 101, before Tony Lewis and Alan Rees batted with freedom to leave the visitors with a tricky target of 268 on the wearing surface.

Jim Pressdee claims the vital wicket of Tom Veivers in the Austrlaians second innings.

By the close of play on the second night, Australia fought back in reaching 75-1, and as the crowd returned home on the Bank Holiday evening, it looked as if their dream of a Welsh victory had evaporated once again. But the following morning, the home side fought back with Shepherd giving little away during an outstanding spell. The youthful Glamorgan side also excelled in the field with Tony Lewis taking a superb running catch in the deep, whilst Alan Rees took a fine catch waist-high at mid-wicket as the tourists slipped to 207-6. Eifion Jones, the reserve wicketkeeper, also made some telling contributions behind the stumps as the pressure became too intense for the Australian tail-enders.

Despite the heat, and a touch or two of cramp, Shepherd and Pressdee continued to infuriate the visitors and as the seventh, eighth and ninth wickets fell, the Glamorgan side - and the crowd of nearly 15,000 - held their breath as history beckoned. With 37 runs still to make, Eifion Jones then caught Neil Hawke, before what seemed like half the population of the Principality surged onto the field and then took part in an unscripted, but very Celtic celebration to rival anything that had taken place on the Eisteddfod *maes* the previous weekend.

The champagne corks popped and speeches were made from the pavilion balcony by Ossie Wheatley and his jubilant Glamorgan team, and as the

The crowd swarms onto the outfield at St. Helen's after Glamorgan clinch their first historic victory over the 1964 Australians.

The crowd start singing the Welsh National Anthem after Ossie Wheatley's team had claimed the final Australian wicket.

songs from supporters in the pavilion and on the outfield grew louder and louder by the minute, it became clear to any doubters that it wasn't just Glamorgan who had beaten the Australians, it was Wales too!

Four years later, Glamorgan became the first county team to beat the Australians on consecutive tours as they defeated the 1968 tourists. By this time Tony Lewis had taken over the captaincy from Wheatley, but the gifted strokemaker was taken ill before the game with the Australians, and it was his trusty lieutenant Don Shepherd who led the side into the field. The subsequent victory was a tribute to Shep's guile and experience, as the visitors struggled again on yet another slow, Swansea wicket.

The surface though had lost some of its spite from previous years, and with less spin, batting was much easier on the St Helen's wicket. After winning the toss and batting first, Glamorgan were indebted to a magnificent 99 from Alan Jones, their fine left-handed opening batsman as they made 224, whilst Majid Khan, their newly recruited batsman from Pakistan made a typically sublime half-century, as Jones remembers:

> "Majid produced an innings which brought the crowd to their feet. He injected a momentum that was badly needed in a game so far characterised by plenty of good cricket but no, what would you say, zest. Majid's fire rekindled my attacking play and soon we had the scoreboard operators working for their money. The mid-afternoon lull was enlivened by 87 runs in 47 minutes. Majid scored 55 - all but nine in boundaries before being stumped by Jarman off Mallett."[3]

As in 1964, the Australians lost cheap wickets on the Saturday evening as

Roger Davis pictured batting against the 1968 Australians at Swansea.

they slipped to 80-6 in the face of clever left-arm bowling from Malcolm Nash who produced some sharp in-swing which, allied to his priceless knack of being able to drift the ball the other way, confounded the illustrious Australian batsmen who yielded a first innings lead of 114 to Shepherd and his merry men.

With the wicket still revealing a benign character, the instructions from the acting captain were for quick runs. Half centuries from Roger Davis and West Indian recruit Bryan Davis helped Glamorgan to extend the lead to 364, before 'Shep' declared to leave the Aussies all of the final day to chase this target. With clear blue skies, the Swansea ground was packed to the rafters shortly before the start of the last day's play, with everyone hoping that the Welsh county could record another famous victory. Alan Jones still remembers Shepherd's words to his team before taking to the field on that fateful day:

> "Don's talk to our team was simple. Give away nothing, field like they have fielded and bowlers just do your job!"[4]

The game in 1968 was very different to the encounter four years before as 'Shep' reasoned that Glamorgan's best chance of winning was for the Australians to think they could get the runs, rather than shutting up shop and blocking out for a draw. Like a Grand Master at chess, the wily spinner cleverly rotated his bowling as the Australians watchfully accumulated against the enthusiastic Glamorgan team, with Paul Sheahan, their number four batsman, recording a fighting century.

But wickets steadily fell, sometimes with bad balls, as Sheahan drilled

Don Shepherd stands proudly at the foot of the pavilion stairs after he had master minded Glamorgan victory over the 1968 Australians.

a poor delivery from Peter Walker straight back to the bowler. With a career tally of 697 first-class victims and a reputation as one of the greatest fielders in the county game, Walker was not going to miss out, and his catch turned the game in Glamorgan's favour. With the lower order exposed, and with the ball starting to turn, there was a flurry of lusty boundaries, but to the delight of the home crowd, the fours and sixes were accompanied by wickets as the razor-sharp Glamorgan fielders held every chance that came their way, and when Dave Renneberg's holed out to Majid, Glamorgan had won by 79 runs.

Welsh hymns were soon echoing around the ground yet again, together with a rendition of 'Waltzing Matilda' before Shepherd and his players addressed the crowd to celebrate another defining moment in Welsh sporting history. After sustained applause for 'Shep' in recognition of his wily captaincy, Barry Jarman – the Australian skipper – also spoke to the crowd and the biggest cheer of the day came when he began by saying "What's new about being beaten by Glamorgan!" The cheering, singing crowd, saluting winning captain Shepherd on the steps in front of the pavilion in 1968 also illustrated the heights to which these fixtures with touring teams aspired.

Don Shepherd and Barry Jarman make impromptu speeches from the pavilion balcony after the Welsh county secured successive victories at the Swansea ground against the Australians.

As Alan Jones remembers:

> "The celebrations in the St, Helen's bar went on all night. We were joined by some of the Pontarddulais Male Voice Choir who rushed down to see us from their base at the Fountain Hotel in the 'Bont' after watching our victory on BBC TV. Normally, we would take guests and opposing teams to the Fountain on a Sunday night to listen after practice sessions.
>
> The following night, they came to see us and how the Aussies enjoyed it! I can still see Barry Jarman even now up on top of a table conducting us all. He was to have caught the 7.30pm train to London; he eventually caught the 8.30 am [the next day]. It was Phil Jones, one of the choir's leaders who suffered most. At lunch on the Bank Holiday Monday, he had told his wife he was just going to the Fountain to get some cigarettes; the next time she saw him was Tuesday morning!"[5]

The crowd swarm onto the outfield as the Australian's second innings comes to an end in their match with Glamorgan at Swansea in 1926.

1. One further rugby international was played at St. Helen's - on 16 November 1997 as Wales beat Tonga 46-12.
2. D.Miller, *Born to Bowl* (Fairfield Books, 2004).
3. A.Jones with T.Stevens, *Hooked on Opening* (Gomer Publishing, 1984).
4. Ibid
5. Ibid

Chapter Fourteen

Sixes at Swansea

"It's the place where six sixes were first hit in an over" - a comment frequently made by first-time visitors to the St. Helen's ground, referring to the record-breaking efforts of Sir Garry Sobers against the occasional left-arm spin of Malcolm Nash whilst batting for Nottinghamshire against Glamorgan at Swansea during a County Championship encounter in 1968.

The Bajan's batting fireworks occurred on 31 August 1968 as Nottinghamshire were manoeuvring their way to setting the Welsh county a target on the final day of the Championship match, under the ever-watchful eye of the BBC Wales TV cameras. Sobers' efforts came against Malcolm Nash - the left-arm swing bowler - at the Pavilion End who was undertaking a spell of left-arm spin, knowing that a declaration was imminent.

Regarded as the finest all-round player in modern cricket, Garry played in 93 Tests for the West Indies, besides playing golf, soccer and basketball for Barbados. When batting the left-hander regularly unleashed a series of elegant and powerful strokes, and many shrewd judges of the game consider Garry's innings of 254 for the Rest of the World against Australia in 1971 to have been one of the finest ever played. If his batting was great, then his bowling was superb, with Garry having a variety of styles, bowling two styles of spin - left-arm orthodox and wrist spin - as well as being a potent fast-medium opening bowler.

Blessed with such natural talents, Garry had made his first-class debut in 1952/53 at the age of sixteen, before making his Test debut the following season against England at Kingston. In 1957/58 he set a world record for the highest score made by an individual batsman in Test cricket by scoring a superb 365* against Pakistan. Lithe and athletic, Garry always played cricket with a smile on his face, and during the County Championship encounter at Swansea in 1968, the left-handed batsman despatched the 23 year-old from Abergavenny for 36 runs in the space of an over.

The first two balls disappeared high over the heads of the mid-wicket fielders and into the crowd sitting in the enclosures, before the third delivery - pushed a little wider on the off-side - was driven by Sobers over long-off and into the seating in front of the historic Pavilion. Nash then dropped the fourth ball a little bit shorter, but Sobers quickly rocked onto the backfoot, and pulled it square of the wicket for another six.

The fifth ball was on a good length around off stump, and Sobers again played a lofted straight drive. But he did not hit the ball quite as cleanly as before, and it travelled high and straight towards Roger Davis on the long-

A montage from the BBC Sport Wales film reels of Garry Sobers' record-breaking blows at Swansea in 1968.

off boundary. The Glamorgan fielder caught the ball, but in so doing, he tumbled backwards over the ropes. Some people thought that Sobers was out, whilst others shouted six as the umpires consulted with the fielders. The MCC had brought in a new regulation regarding such situations at the start of the 1968 season, stating that a fielder had to remain within the playing area for a catch to be made, so after a quick chat, the umpires signalled six again.

As Nash regathered the ball and pondered where to put the last delivery, Eifion Jones – the Glamorgan wicketkeeper – jokingly said to Sobers: "Bet you can't hit this one for six as well." The West Indian simply turned around and grinned, took guard and then ferociously despatched the ball like a rocket high over mid-wicket for his sixth six and a place in the cricket record books.

Garry later recalled his thought processes ahead of facing that historic sixth ball:

> "As Malcolm prepared to bowl... I reasoned that he would try to change his pace and maybe bowl a quicker ball. All my previous five shots had been the same. A change of pace might bring about a mishit and a catch. A modern bowler, with years of experience bowling in one-day matches, might well have drilled a quicker ball in on my toes, one of the most difficult deliveries to hit for six. But Malcolm was trying to get me out. He was an attacking bowler. The ball dropped short on middle stump and I connected in the middle of the bat." [1]

Nottinghamshire's declaration followed soon afterwards and, as Peter Walker remembers:

> "Alongside a beaming Nash, [Garry] walked off to a standing ovation. As they drew level with me, I overheard the game's most charismatic and accomplished all-rounder ask Malcolm how he could be so cheerful after what had just happened to him? It was typical of Nash to reply:

Malcolm Nash in more happier times at Swansea as he receives a presentation from the St. Helen's Balconiers.

> 'Well Garry, we're now together in the world record books, and you couldn't have done it without me!'
>
> In the dressing room, Malcolm had often expressed the view that given the chance. He could be as good a slow bowler as any in the country. Never short of self-confidence and irrespective of the state of the game, he always wanted the ball in his hand. Not for nothing had we nicknamed Malcolm, whose initials were M.A.N. - superman!"[2]

Almost nine years later to the day, Nash was also on the receiving end again - this time in normal seam and swing mode from the Mumbles Road End - as Lancashire's Frank Hayes struck him for 34 runs in an over during their Championship match at Swansea. The onslaught by the visiting batsman took place straight after lunch on the second day as Glamorgan took the new ball in Lancashire's second innings. The first delivery from Nash disappeared over long-leg as Hayes pulled a short ball to the ropes before the second was driven square of the wicket for four.

Four maximums then followed as Hayes deposited Nash high over mid-wicket and onto Gorse Lane for six, before the next ball was nonchalantly clipped over long-on for six. The fifth ball of this eventful over was then planted over the head of the fielder at long-off and into the seating in the Rugby Grandstand before the final ball, accompanied by huge cheers from the Lancashire contingent, clattered into the scoreboard positioned on the embankment beyond the ropes at mid-wicket.

This time there were just brief handshakes from the Glamorgan fielders to Hayes as the fielders swopped positions at the end of an over which had nearly given the watching journalists some memorable copy as the Lancashire man came within two runs of equalling Sobers' feats. Understandably the writers were eager to find out Nash's thoughts so a hasty press conference was called. They need not have worries as Nash duly gave them a golden line for their reports. With a wry grin on his face, he quipped "it was nearly a case of *déjà vu* and now it's happened to me from both ends of the ground. Not many people can say that!"[3]

The major difference with 1968 was that Hayes' run-spree had come without the television cameras being present and no photographers recorded his feat, blow-by-blow. In contrast, Sobers' fusillade was captured for posterity by BBC Wales, but only with a huge slice of luck. After undertaking a live broadcast earlier in the afternoon, the producer and camera crew agreed to continue filming the game.

Ever since the early 1960s, BBC Wales had been covering Glamorgan's matches at Swansea, with the coverage of Championship and tourist matches also being used by the Corporation as an opportunity to train camera crews from other regions. On this particular afternoon, the producer/director John Norman had initially told the cameramen to stand down but one of them, John Lewis, asked if he could stay on. Norman agreed and asked Wilf Wooller, the legendary Glamorgan captain, who was providing the commentary to stay on as well in case something should happen which could be used in a highlights programme the following day.

The view of St. Helen's from the BBC TV gantry erected together with commentary boxes at the Mumbles Road End.

A message was also sent to the technical team near St. Mary's Hill in Bridgend who were relaying the signals back to Broadcasting House in Cardiff and who were also supposed to go on a break. This completely *ad hoc* decision meant that this very special piece of cricket history was recorded for posterity, together with Wooller's excited description of the last six: "And it's gone all the way down to Swansea." The first airing of the footage came towards the end of *Grandstand*, and shortly afterwards, the early evening news, whilst the BBC authorities also arranged for a post-match interview between Brian Hoey, their news presenter and the two record-breaking cricketers.

Radio commentary of matches had taken place at Swansea since the late 1920s. The Swansea Wireless Relay Station had been opened in December 1924 with the 110 foot aerial on Town Hill allowing the town's Mayor to undertake the first broadcast from the newly completed studios in what he described as "the capital of West Wales."[4]

The coverage of cricket and rugby matches at St. Helen's had also been encouraged from this time by Gerald Cock, the BBC's first-ever Director of Outside Broadcasts, especially as it was a highly effective way of filling the transmission schedules and was a way of not over burdening the fairly limited studios. Appointed in 1925, Cock soon began overseeing innovative coverage of sporting events, as well as the introduction of new technology in transmitting reports and action commentary from a number of sporting venues across the UK, including the Arms Park and St. Helen's.

To facilitate the coverage of matches, Cock issued instructions that the BBC should provide financial assistance so that proper facilities could be provided for its commentators. Therefore, 150 guineas was given to the

Garry Sobers and Malcolm Nash are interviewed by Brian Hoey of BBC Wales after play on the day of the record-breaking over during Glamorgan's Championship match against Nottinghamshire.

WRU in order to create an improved broadcast facility at the Arms Park, whilst in 1930 Swansea Cricket and Football Club received £25 for similar facilities in the new pavilion which had been created at St. Helen's.[5]

There were some though who felt that the Beeb could provide more cash, especially when their coverage could have an adverse effect on gate takings. Things came to a head in 1934 as planning began for live coverage of Glamorgan's match against the Australian tourists. It soon became clear that the facilities were rather limited and that greater space on the pavilion roof was needed. In June 1934 Robert Palmer, the Secretary of Swansea Cricket and Football Club duly wrote to the BBC asking for greater financial support.

A terse reply followed from the Programme Director, West Regional Office saying that the BBC felt they had already supported the club, that their broadcasting position was rather poor and they were not getting what they thought they deserved. The Programme Director also wrote to Cock saying "I am all for doling out a little money if anything is to come from it, but I do want to warn you that the story is likely to be a serial rather than a short. For example, the Glamorgan County Cricket Club is perennially hat in hand and on the verge of bankruptcy."[6]

After further correspondence, an amicable solution was reached, with further financial assistance being given so that a better commentary position was established for both the cricket and rugby matches. During the post-war era, the involvement of Wilf Wooller, the Glamorgan captain, in the coverage of matches helped to build an effective link with the

JBG Thomas commentates, whilst Cliff Morgan peers through the binoculars from the BBC commentary position on the roof of the Swansea pavilion in 1964.

county cricket club and the national broadcaster with Wilf acting as lead commentator, and also the presenter of *Sports Line Up*, the BBC Wales' sports review programme.

The involvement of the BBC through their radio and television broadcasts allowed a wider number of people to hear about, and see the delights of cricket at the Swansea ground, and over the years, a number of leading broadcasters have extolled the virtues of St. Helen's, not least John Arlott who in the years immediately after the Second World War enjoyed his visits to the ground where he met up frequently with his good friend, the poet Dylan Thomas.

Arlott had been a supporter of Glamorgan Cricket from the early 1930s. With his boyhood hero being Maurice Turnbull, the self-styled 'Basingstoke Boy' had travelled with a friend by bicycle and train to Cardiff to watch Turnbull bat at the Arms Park against Nottinghamshire in the closing game of the 1932 season. With Harold Larwood and Bill Voce in their ranks, the visitors experimented with Bodyline bowling ahead of the winter tour to Australia: to Arlott's delight Turnbull's response was a fine double-hundred and a record stand with Dai Davies as the England bowlers were put to sword. As he later wrote, "the ultimate assessment of that innings is that Larwood eventually ceased to drop short or to bowl at his leg stump."[7]

After the War, Arlott succeeded George Orwell as the BBC's producer of the weekly *Book of Verse* series for the Overseas Service. Through his work for the programme between 1945 and 1950, and his contact with poets, he developed a close friendship with Dylan Thomas, and as David Rayvern-Allen later wrote:

> "As country lads together in the smoke, Arlott and Thomas drank together, argued together, aspired and conspired together. With Celtic wives and family back in distant Hampshire and Carmarthenshire, there were times when they even shared a house together." [8]

Thomas loved cricket, as well as watching rugby, drinking beer, telling jokes and writing poetry. As Arlott later wrote, he was a delight to work with as a radio producer, not least because "he was a man with a voice that uttered poetry with the quality of a bugle note."[9] John would always contact Dylan when he was posted by the BBC to commentate on Glamorgan's matches. On one occasion when covering a game at the Arms Park, the pair met up after play and visited Tiger Bay, where they listened to, and were struck by, the potential of a young female singer called Shirley Bassey. But the pair were happiest when Glamorgan visited St. Helen's, with Arlott writing how Thomas :

> "would turn up at county matches at Swansea, and curl up quietly in a corner of the commentary box, living it all through and then afterwards came away to one of the pubs or restaurants of his friends who received him so gladly. The evening invariably ended in sheer contentment, if not utter sobriety."[10]

It was from the commentary box on the roof-top at Swansea that Arlott penned the following, entitled *"Cricket at Swansea: Glamorgan in the Field"*, although it is interesting to speculate how many of these stanza's originated from his good friend[11]:

From the top of the hill-top pavilion,
The sea is a cheat to the eye
Where it secretly seeps into coastline
Or fades in the fellow-grey sky,
But the creasemarks are clear on the green
As the axe's first taste of the tree,
And sharp is the Welshmen's assault
As the freshening fret from the sea.
The ball is a withering weapon,
Fraught with a strong-fingered spin
And the fieldsmen, with fingers prehensile,
Are the arms of attack moving in,
For the catch is their new Cymric mission,

With outcricket cruel as a cat
To pounce on the perilous snick
As it breaks on the spin-harried bat.

On this turf the remembered of rugby,
"The Invincibles", came by their name,
And now, in the calm of the clubhouse,
Frown down from their old-fashioned frame.
Their might has outlived their moustaches,
For photos fade faster than fame;
And his cricket rekindles the temper
Of their high trampling, scrummaging game:
As intense as an Eisteddfod anthem
It burns down the day like a flame.

Eifion Jones catches Bob Taylor, watched by Peter Walker in their Championship match against Derbyshire at Swansea in 1970.

1. G.Sobers with B.Scovell: *Twenty Years at The Top* (Macmillan, 1998).
2. P.M.Walker, *It's not just Cricket* (Fairfield Books, 2006).
3. *Western Mail*, 30 August 1977.
4. D.Farmer, *The Life and Times of Swansea RFC* (DFPS, 1995).
5. Drawn from notes in the BBC Written Archives Centre in Reading. File R30/3572/1 Welsh Rugby Union (Outside Broadcasts), 1927-1939. Thanks to Dr. Daryl Leeworthy for his assistance with this research.
6. Ibid.
7. J.Arlott, *Basingstoke Boy: The Autobiography* (Fontana, London,1992).
8. David Rayvern-Allen quoted on www.cricketweb.net/forum/cricket-chat/5434-dylan-thomas-john-arlott.html
9. J.Arlott, op.cit.
10. Ibid
11. Published in the Bishop Gore School CC Tercentenary Brochure, published for their Cricket Festival in July 1982.

Chapter Fifteen

International cricket comes to Swansea

Bringing international cricket to Wales had always been one of the founding principles upon which Glamorgan CCC came into being during a meeting of the great and the good of the cricket world in South Wales at The Angel Hotel in Cardiff in July 1888. Within a few years, they had entered the Minor County Championship and were joint winners of the competition in 1900, as the Club's committee gleefully discussed how the game could be further developed across South Wales.

Flushed by their success in the Minor County competition, Glamorgan attempted to host the opening Test of the 1905 England-Australia series, but their bid to host a match at Cardiff failed by the slender margin of one vote, and it was to be over six decades later that the administrators eventually allocated international cricket to Wales. The match in question was the one-day international in July 1973 between England and New Zealand at the St. Helen's ground.

Ray Illingworth leads out the England team at Swansea for their Prudential Trophy Match with New Zealand in July 1973.

The early 1970s had seen the introduction of one-day internationals into the summer schedule with England playing their first limited-overs match against Australia in Melbourne in January 1971, with the 40 overs a side contest arranged after the Test Match at the same ground had been washed out without a ball being bowled. During the Australians visit to the UK in 1972, three one-day internationals were included in the schedule, and the following summer, more were added, including the match in the Prudential Trophy between England and New Zealand.

The allocation of the game to Swansea followed an extensive period of lobbying to the games authorities by Wilf Wooller who argued that this new format of cricket should be allocated to different venues than the traditional ones used for Test Matches, and grounds such as Swansea, which had a reputation for decent crowds. As the Glamorgan Secretary wrote at the time:

> "Following the introduction of one-day internationals into the domestic schedule, I lobbied the Test and County Cricket Board that these games should be held at venues which did not currently host Test Matches, but had a tradition for attracting handsome crowds for county games.
>
> The one-day internationals were a new and different type of cricket, so I was pleased when the TCCB agreed with my premise that a game in the 1973 Prudential Trophy series with New Zealand should go to a new and different venue. I was even more delighted when their choice for the game on 18th July was Swansea. A crowd of just over 10,000 turned up and the gross gate was £4,114."[1]

This was a decent outcome because rain had threatened to play havoc with the game, with the pre-match preparations being blighted by unseasonal rain. As JBG Thomas wrote in the *Western Mail*:

> "A lot of sun is needed to make the first Test [sic] cricket match played in Wales at Swansea a success. The St. Helen's pitch has received a real soaking but sun and the quick drying properties of the sandy sub-soil will, it is hoped, ensure a fine match."[2]

The fact that there was a decent gate was gratifying for the Glamorgan authorities who had spent around £4,00 on ensuring the ground was up to standard for the international contest, with a new scoreboard erected at the top of the bank on the eastern side and replacing the two-sided structure adjacent to Gorse Lane, besides building a new press box next to the Pavilion and erecting five marquees on the rugby pitch in order to provide dining and catering facilities for the crowd, VIP guests and sponsors.

The game was staged at Swansea eight days after the three-Test series had ended by the margin of two games to one in favour of Ray Illingworth's England side. The two matches for the Prudential Trophy were staged at Swansea and Manchester over the course of three days in mid-July, and with bad weather at Old Trafford, it was just the game at St. Helen's which reached a positive outcome, with a century by Warwickshire's Dennis

Amiss propelling England to a comprehensive victory by seven wickets.

For the umpteenth time in the ground's history, batting proved to be difficult on an overcast morning after the Kiwis had opted to bat first. With the new ball pairing of John Snow and Geoff Arnold finding conditions very much in their favour, the New Zealanders slumped to 15-4. Glenn Turner and Vic Pollard mounted a recovery mission, adding 55 in 21 overs during a partnership which was staid in modern terms but, at the time, did much to stabilise the tourists innings with Pollard completing a defiant fifty besides remining at the crease until the 44th over.

Richard Hadlee used the long handle to good effect as the Kiwis ended on 158 after 52.5 overs, but their efforts were put into context as Geoff Boycott and Amiss added 96 for the first wicket and revelled in the easier batting conditions. Amiss was the aggressor as he raced to his century inside 39 overs, but was fortunate when on 37 to be dropped at extra cover by the normally dependent Pollard. Despite being dismissed with his side were in sight of their target, Amiss' volley of well-timed drives were enough to win the Warwickshire batsman the Man of the Match Award.

As JBG Thomas highlighted in his match report for the *Western Mail*, there were others who had played a hand in England's comprehensive win, but Amiss' innings had been the stand-out performance, especially as his flurry of boundaries had put Geoff Boycott in the shade:

> "Hostile and devastating pace bowling by Snow and Arnold had set the tone before a brilliant century from Dennis Amiss who displayed scintillating form to guide England safely and attractively to victory, even outshining an extremely subdued Geoff Boycott who never got going."[3]

Cyril Walters, as the first Welshman to captain England in Test cricket, presented Amiss with his Man of the Match Award and said "we are all grateful to the authorities for bringing the England side to Wales for the first time. I hope they will do it frequently in the future!"[4]

But it was to be a further ten years before Swansea staged its next international cricket, in the year when the 1983 World Cup was staged in the UK with a number of county grounds, not on the normal international schedule staging the 60-overs a side contests.

The opening batch of group games on 9 June saw Pakistan meet Sri Lanka at Swansea as together with Taunton, Leicester, Bristol, Worcester, Southampton, Derby, Tunbridge Wells and Chelmsford, group games in the competition were staged at a number of non-Test match venues. As in the previous international game, the unique micro-climate of the Swansea ground played a role with Pakistan put into bat after early morning rain. Sri Lanka opened with Vincent John, a burly medium-fast bowler, but not fast enough to cause Mohsin Khan and Zaheer Abbas to swap their green-starred Pakistan caps for helmets.

After John hit Mohsin's middle stump with a yorker, Javed Miandad, contracted at the time to Glamorgan, came to the middle with his arrival greeted by a roar of approval from local supporters as well as those supporting Pakistan. Javed's partnership with Zaheer built on the good work of the earlier batsmen with Zaheer, better known as an off-side player, hooking and rolling his wrists on the ball as he despatched it into the leg-side. With bright, hot sunshine bathing the ground their efforts had seen Pakistan to 187 off 44 overs with Zaheer driving fluently, besides securing an all-run four to deep square-leg to expose some shoddy fielding by the Sri Lankans.

Zaheer eventually departed in the 50th over before Imran Khan came in to provide the coup de grace, striking 56 from just 33 balls as he feasted on the tiring attack. Javed joined in with the run spree striking 49 from 24 balls with a pair of massive sixes into the member's enclosure before departing leg before as Pakistan added 108 from the last ten overs.

Majid Khan receives an award.

Sri Lanka's task was to score 339 on what had become a very flat wicket, but the loss of wickets at frequent intervals prevented any meaningful partnerships from taking place. All of the Pakistan seamers found conditions in their favour, including Rashid Khan, the black-haired young bowler, whose self-conscious smile peeped out from behind a small but bushy black beard. Right from his opening over, he got the ball to swing as the tide advanced out in Swansea Bay as the Sri Lankan batsmen played and missed.

There was a glimmer of hope for the Ceylonese as nineteen year-old Arjuna Ranatunga, with a build like a heavyweight boxer, threatened to mount a spirited riposte. He had been compared with Garry Sobers, and been coached by Sobers, and now - at the ground where the West Indian maestro had written his name in to the game's record books - he batted like him, effortlessly driving Tahir Naqqash through extra cover before smashing another ball back so hard that umpire David Shepherd had to dive out of the way.

His efforts had taken the score to 142 in the 34th over, before two Sri Lankans were run out whilst Ranatunga was caught and bowled by Mudassar Nazar. Their lower order, led by Guy de Alwis, gleefully tried to make amends but the task of scoring at ten or eleven an over was well beyond them as Pakistan - at 8.15pm in the evening - completed a victory by 50 runs.

No more international cricket has taken place at the ground since this contest, and with changes to the domestic calendar, fewer touring teams have been visiting Swansea either over the August Bank Holiday or at other times of the year. The changes to the programme began during the mid-1960s, with 1964 being the final season when the Australians played a pair of Bank Holiday fixtures, appearing at the Arms Park over Whitsun and playing at Swansea in August. 1965 saw New Zealand visiting the Arms Park at Whitsun whilst the Springboks filled the August slot at St. Helen's, but in 1966 there was just a solitary game against the West Indians at Swansea. There were two tours again in 1967 with Pakistan playing in Swansea whilst the Indians were involved in the inaugural fixture at the club's new ground in Cardiff at Sophia Gardens.

A view of St. Helen's in 1985 with its extended pavilion and clubhouse.

1968 saw the historic game at Swansea against the Australians over the August Bank Holiday but with pressure for shorter itineraries and Bill Lawry's team arriving later than any Australian team had done before, there was only one match. In 1969 there was a return to twin tours but the tourist game at Swansea, against the West Indians, took place in early July whilst Sophia Gardens staged the match with the New Zealanders over the August Bank Holiday.

If the scheduling of tourist games at Swansea and Cardiff saw the resurfacing of the east-west tensions in the committee room, it was global politics, or more correctly the anti-apartheid movement which affected the matches in 1970. The South Africans had been scheduled to play at Swansea during the last week of July. But the tour was cancelled and through the efforts of the Glamorgan committee, and in particular Bill Edwards, the proprietor of the sports shop in King Edward's Road, the fixture was taken up by Jamaica.

His links with the Caribbean administrators saw further changes to the format of the tourist games at Swansea during the 1970s with lucrative one-day games, mirroring the Sunday League competition, being staged against the West Indians on their tours in 1973, 1976 and 1980. A similar venture was planned in July 1982 when the Pakistanis visited Swansea, with Bill using his close links with their officials to secure a 40-over match on the Sunday afternoon, but the weather conspired against them as the contest was washed out.

The 1980s saw another important change with Glamorgan securing a deal with the Neath Development Partnership to stage the matches against the 1985, 1989 and 1993 Australians at The Gnoll. With generous sponsorship from those involved in the industrial regeneration of the area, these contests drew decent-sized crowds, with the Pakistani duo of Javed Miandad and Younis Ahmed also sharing a triple-century stand in the 1985 contest.

Ten years before, it was fellow Pakistani Majid Khan who played the last great innings by a Glamorgan batsman against the Australians at St. Helen's, with Majid playing an innings during which this consumate batsman teased and taunted a world-clas attack all over the field, racing to fifty in just 47 minutes, with ten sweetly-struck fours. The bowlers he decimated were Alan Hurst, Max Walker, Gary Gilmour, Ashley Mallett and Ian Chappell - perhaps not the greatest Australian attack of all time, but it was the manner in which Majid majestically made his century. His innings also followed a fine opening stand as Alan Jones and his teenage colleague, Alan Lewis Jones, put on 132 for the first wicket with the youngster, wearing a white floppy sunhat, showing great promise for the future with an innings which belied his youthful eagerness.

As the two Joneses sent the ball time and again to the boundary, and Majid gracefully devoured the Australian attack, many in the sun-drenched crowd fancifully looked forward to further great days for Glamorgan's cricketers at Swansea and further victories by the next generation of Welsh

Jeff Jones seen bowling at St. Helen's during Glamorgan's Championship match with Worcestershire in 1968. Alan Ormrod is the batsman, Eifion Jones the wicketkeeper, with Majid Khan and Roger Davis in the slips.

cricketers over touring teams at St. Helen's. But the 1980s and 1990s saw the gradual end of tourist matches in Swansea. The 1988 West Indians visited Swansea in mid-August, but this time there was not a limited overs contest in the schedule. Two years later, the Indians visited at the same time of the year, before the 1991 West Indians returned in mid-July for what has turned out to be their last visit to St. Helen's with their itinerary in 2000 seeing the contest take place at Sophia Gardens.

Indeed, the 1990s saw Glamorgan switch the tourist fixtures to the Cardiff ground as they took the first steps on the path towards creating a modern stadium. Sophia Gardens duly hosted Glamorgan's matches against the 1997 Australians and 1998 Sri Lankans, whilst the 1999 ICC World Cup saw the Australians based in the Welsh capital. The tournament schedule saw Glamorgan take part in warm-up games against Australia and Kenya, before a group game in the competition between Australia and New Zealand which the Kiwi's won thanks to some forthright batting by former Warwickshire batsman Roger Twose.

This was the first one-day international at Glamorgan's headquarters as the focus of international attention switched from west to east, with games against the 2000 West Indians and 2002 Sri Lankans taking place at Sophia Gardens. Pontypridd had also dipped their toe briefly in the waters, with financial backing from Mid-Glamorgan County Council, and latterly administrators within the Rhondda Cynon Taff authority seeing Ynysangharad Park host matches between Glamorgan and the South Africans in 1994, followed two years later by a match against the Pakistanis.

The view from the boundary at The Gnoll in 1985 as Neath plays host to Glamorgan's game against the Australians.

With changes and congestion in the international schedule, full season tours by overseas teams are now a thing of the past, and although Swansea staged games against the A teams from India and Sri Lanka in 2003 and again in 2004, the last three-day game against a full international side at Swansea took place in mid-June 1994 with the visit of the New Zealanders to St. Helen's.

The Kiwis were on English and Welsh soil from early May until late June during which time they had a three-Test series against England, plus a pair of one-day internationals. The game with Glamorgan began on 8th June, just a couple of days after they had suffered an innings defeat in the opening Test at Trent Bridge, where Graham Gooch had struck a masterly double-century and Phil de Freitas had taken the bowling honours.

With the second Test the following week at Lord's, the New Zealanders had games at Swansea and against Gloucestershire at Bristol in which to find form. They duly recorded an eight-wicket victory over Glamorgan in a contest where Hugh Morris had invited the tourists to chase a target of 305 from 70 overs on the final day. For some of the romantics in the crowd, the declaration evoked memories of the Australian match in 1968 but 10 June 1994 was not to be another great date in Welsh sporting history as a 71-ball century by Ken Rutherford saw the tourists canter home with four overs to spare. As Phil Blanche wrote in the *Western Mail*:

"The New Zealand captain upstaged world record holder Brian Lara to hammer the fastest century of the season. Rutherford took just 45 balls to reach 50 with Robert Croft and Steve Bastien in particular being punished severely. Rutherford went on to reach a chanceless century with four sixes and eleven fours before retiring hurt with hamstring injury."[5]

For a ground steeped in history, Swansea did lead the way as far as Glamorgan was concerned with floodlit cricket as six floodlit contests were staged at St. Helen's as the Welsh county, like their counterparts in England, took its first tentative step on the road towards day-night games. The inaugural floodlit game took place on 3 August 1988 with the rugby ground's floodlit pylons illuminating an all-weather pitch laid out on the rugby field, with Glamorgan meeting a star-studded Rest of the World XI as part of the Club's centenary year celebrations.

The venture was repeated on an annual basis for the next five years but the contests against the Rest of the World side, staged on the artificial surface and with tiny straight boundaries were something of a gimmick rather than being serious cricketing fare with rain, rather appropriately, washing out the final scheduled game on 13 July 1993.

Given its superior capacity over the Sophia Gardens ground, St. Helen's was the venue for most of Glamorgan's quarter-final and semi-final contests in one-day games until the late 1990s. Indeed, it was at Swansea in August

A view of the floodlit cricket on the rugby field at St. Helen's.

A view of the Swansea ground in 1990.

1977 that Glamorgan, after three damp days, defeated Leicestershire in the Gillette Cup semi-final to clinch a place at a Lord's final for the first-ever time. June 2005 also saw a Twenty20 match at St. Helen's as Glamorgan met Warwickshire, but this remains the only game in the all-action competition staged at Swansea as, like all of the Welsh county's other major games, they are staged at the Club's headquarters in Cardiff.

1. Taken from a manuscript for an article, believed to have been unpublished, written by Wilf Wooller for the *Sunday Telegraph* in 1979.
2. *Western Mail*, 18 July 1973.
3. *Western Mail*, 19 July 1973
4. Ibid.
5. *Western Mail*, 11 June 1994.

Chapter Sixteen

Rapid hundreds, remarkable debuts and great run outs

There's not been an innings quite like it at St. Helen's, and probably there will never be one to equal the feats of Clive Lloyd at Swansea during the long hot summer of 1976 as the West Indian tourists met Glamorgan over the August Bank Holiday weekend. Tales of Garry Sobers' six sixes in 1968 and other big-hitting feats paled into insignificance as, in the course of two hours on a balmy Monday, the tourist's captain equalled Gilbert Jessop's world-record for the fastest-ever double hundred in first-class cricket.

During the space of just two hours of cricketing mayhem, the West Indian batsman struck an unbeaten 201 after Gordon Greenidge and Viv Richards had also recorded scintillating hundreds during the morning session. After reaching a relatively sober hundred from 79 balls, Lloyd accelerated in brutal fashion during the early afternoon, reaching his double-hundred just 45 balls later as he put to the sword the left-arm spin of England aspirant Tony Allin as well as Barry Lloyd's off-breaks plus the seam of Rodney Ontong, Tony Cordle and Malcolm Nash.

Clive Lloyd, the tormentor of Glamorgan in 1976, seen six years before leaving the outfield at Sophia Gardens after a Sunday League game with Glamorgan.

None of the bowlers could contain the left-handed batsman from Guyana with viewers of the match, being broadcast on BBC Wales TV, left unsure whether they were watching the highlights or viewing live footage, such was the frequency of balls being struck to, or over, the boundary ropes by the West Indian maestro.

"Never before has there been such a display of brutal, yet graceful stroke-play," was the verdict of Ron Griffiths, the long-serving correspondent of the *South Wales Evening Post*. "Hurricane hitting" and "a whirlwind of brutal stroke-play" were the other descriptions coined by Fleet Street journalists from the confines of the small but homely press-box situated at the top of the enclosures at the Pavilion End as Lloyd's remarkable double hundred unfolded with as the tourists rattling up 554-4 in just 83.3 overs before the Lancashire batsman declared in mid-afternoon.

It also proved to be the final game when Majid Khan, the graceful and gifted Pakistani batsman, appeared for the Welsh county. 1976 was far from being one of Glamorgan's finest seasons, with the Club finishing at the bottom of the Championship table, losing 10 of their 20 matches, in addition to finishing in 16th place of the Sunday League table, with just five wins from sixteen games. Having already handed over the captaincy to Alan Jones, Majid made 21 in the first innings before opening the batting when Glamorgan batted again, making 22 before being bowled by Michael Holding

Majid's elevation up the order in the second innings stemmed from the incapacitation of Tyrone Powell, who was making his first-class debut for the Welsh county. He had been dismissed by the fearsome pace of Wayne Daniel from the third ball he faced in the first innings, before being laid low by a stomach upset. But he duly registered a pair in perhaps the most

The luckless, and runless, Tyrone Powell.

arduous of situations a Glamorgan debutant has ever faced, as at number eight in the second innings, he was bowled tenth ball by Holding, yet again without having scored a run.

Nine years later the St. Helen's ground was the scene of a very contrasting debut in first-class cricket for a young Glamorgan batsman as Matthew Maynard burst onto the county scene at Swansea with a century on his first appearance in the County Championship. Born in Lancashire, and raised at Menai Bridge in North Wales, Maynard initially had a short spell on Kent's staff, before joining Glamorgan in 1985. He made his first appearance for the county's 1st XI during the last week of August having been selected in the side for both the Championship and Sunday League match against Yorkshire at the St. Helen's ground.

A washout on the opening day of the three-day fixture meant that Maynard's first innings came on Sunday 25August with the youngster, batting at number five in the order, scoring a composed 18 as Glamorgan made 138 in a game reduced by rain and a sea fret to 29 overs per side. It proved to be a winning total as Yorkshire were restricted to 93-8 chasing an amended target of 96 after a further nine overs were lost to the unseasonal weather.

Two days later, Maynard found himself in the middle again, this time in a first-class contest as Glamorgan were set a target of 272 after further rain prompted an early declaration in the Glamorgan first innings and the forfeiture of Yorkshire's second. He arrived with Glamorgan in a reasonably healthy position at 120-3 but the canny spin of Phil Carrick filleted the middle order. As Maynard later reflected:

A view of the Swansea ground in 1985.

> "In those days, Glamorgan were not use to winning, and we slid from 127-5 to 166-8. There was no pressure on me, so I decided to enjoy myself and play my natural game. David Bairstow, had already kept chirping from behind the stumps 'This one only plays by numbers, he'll not last long'. But by the time Phil North, our last man, was at the wicket, I had gone past fifty, and when I got to 84, Phil played out a maiden over – to a massive round of applause from the crowd who were willing me on to get a hundred."[1]

It was not though a case of the nervous nineties for Maynard as, in the next over, he completed an audacious hundred. Having opted to play his natural game he unleashed some flowing drives on both sides of the wicket. But with fellow debutant Phil North who had been chosen for his abilities as a spinner rather than as a batsman at the other end, Maynard knew that he had to take every opportunity, and in true cavalier fashion, he duly breezed through to three figures with three sixes off successive balls from Carrick. As the teenager later reflected in his memoirs:

> "I knew that with no more wickets in hand, I was not going to get my century by pushing the ball around. The field was set so deep to offer me the single and get Phil on strike, and with virtually every fielder on the boundary, fours were hard to come by.
>
> Phil Carrick was bowling and I decided to hit him over the top. I came down the wicket to his second ball [of the over] and sent it over the sightscreen. It was premeditated. The next ball I did the same thing. I didn't quite hit it right and it only just cleared long-on. I was hitting towards the pavilion, which is the slightly longer of the straight boundaries at St. Helen's, but it was in Championship terms relatively short.
>
> Carrick was a wily bowler and I, a novice at 19, tried to read his mind. I decided that he would not expect me to come down the wicket a third time to him – so I did. The ball went a long way. I had become the youngest Glamorgan player to hit a century [in the Championship] and the first to do so on debut since Frank Pinch in 1921."[2]

Later that over his dream debut ended as he turned down the offer of a single into the covers off the fifth ball, before attempting to cut the last delivery through backward point. He proceeded to guide it straight into the hands of the fielder standing deep in the gully and departed for 102. Glamorgan had lost by 35 runs but Maynard walked off to a standing ovation from the admiring spectators, and soon afterwards, the champagne corks were popping in the Glamorgan changing room. As Maynard later admitted:

> "It was a strange feeling: everyone was cheering but we had lost a match. It took a while for what I had achieved to sink in and much was made of my hitting three consecutive sixes to reach the three-figure mark. I had hit five in all, plus thirteen fours in a 98-ball innings and what was important to me was that, despite the fact it was my first Championship knock, I had played my natural game.

Geoff Boycott came into our dressing-room and came up to me, ignoring everyone else and shook my hand. "Well played, lad" he said and walked off. It was a simple gesture, something he did not have to do, and it meant a lot to me."[3]

Matthew Maynard is congratulated by Rodney Ontong in the changing rooms after his remarkable debut hundred at Swansea in 1985.

If Swansea was the scene of Maynard's scintillating start as a county cricketer, it was, three years later, the place he would rather forget as he was dismissed in bizarre fashion in Glamorgan's Benson and Hedges semi-final against Derbyshire, just when it looked like the young tyro was leading Glamorgan to a place in the final of the competition at Lord's.

To the delight of all concerned, Glamorgan were marking their Centenary Year in 1988 with a decent run in the Benson and Hedges Cup, with Maynard making a fine century in the quarter-final against Nottinghamshire at Sophia Gardens with his 108 seeing Glamorgan home by six wickets and earnt him the Man of the Match Award.

His efforts saw the Welsh county reached the last four of the 55-overs competition and a home tie against Derbyshire at Swansea, leading many - especially those with a romantic persuasion - to speculate whether the Club would mark their anniversary year with another visit to a showpiece one-day final. But during the semi-final Maynard went from hero to zero, just as he appeared to be guiding his team to their first Lord's final since 1977 as the Welsh county were chasing a target of 218.

After the loss of early wickets, Maynard stabilised the innings but just as the Swansea supporters were clearing their throats for renditions of the Welsh National Anthem, a short ball from Welsh Indian fast bowler

Michael Holding saw Maynard move suddenly onto the back foot, with his helmet falling onto his stumps. He departed "hit wicket" and as the crest-fallen batsman later recalled, this turned out to be a turning point in the game, as the visitors went on to secure victory:

> "I was going so well, but then as I played a back foot drive to Holding, my helmet fell off and rolled onto the stumps - something that had never happened before or since! I kept the helmet and the newspaper photographs of the incident, and then in my Benefit Year, I raffled them for what turned out to be a quite tidy sum during a Dinner at the Brangwyn Hall."[4]

Other remarkable hundreds have been scored at Swansea, including an extraordinary and unbeaten 141 by Worcestershire's Glenn Turner at St.

Matthew Maynard's helmet falls onto the stumps in Glamorgan's match with Derbyshire at Swansea in 1988.

Helen's in 1977 with the Kiwi scoring 83.43% of his team's runs. At Swansea in 1975 Turner had made an unbeaten 154 in Worcestershire's total of 300-2 declared, but his efforts two years later were on a completely different scale as the rest of his colleagues mustered a mere 28 runs between them as the visitors were dismissed for 169.

They also came as the visitors were facing the spectre of following-on, with Glamorgan having made 309-4 and then reducing Worcestershire to 93-8 in the unseasonably cold and overcast conditions with spectators huddled up in blankets and duffle coats. But they had plenty of opportunities to clap their hands and stay warm as Turner produced an amazing one-man show, hitting a six and 18 fours during an astonishing innings in which he gave a solitary chance as on 92 he edged Malcolm Nash to second slip where the cold weather may have played a role in Rodney Ontong failing to complete the catch.

As John Billot reported the next day in the *Western Mail*:

> "There have not been many more spectacular instances of complete monopoly of scoring. St. Helen's was one man's kingdom as the 30 year-old New Zealander batted for three hours and forty minutes. As he later explained 'as each batsman came out to join me I spoke a few words to try and help give him confidence.' But it was more like the Mummy's curse because not one of his team-mates reached double figures. Astonishingly the next highest score was skipper Norman Gifford's seven runs!"[5]

Whilst Turner's efforts were - and remain - a world record for the highest percentage of runs by a single batsman in a first-class match, there is nothing in the games annals about Tom Moody's innings at Swansea in July 1990. The tall Australian blasted a century for Warwickshire in the space of just 26 minutes on the final morning of their three-day Championship match as the two captains - Alan Butcher and Andy Lloyd - tried to manufacture a positive outcome from the game. Faced by the occasional spin of Tony Cottey and some gentle lobs from Matthew Maynard, Moody raced to his half-century inside 11 minutes before reaching three figures a quarter of an hour later.

With Maynard conceding 89 runs in his six overs of flighted filth and Cottey 49 from his six, Moody's efforts are not recognised by the games statisticians as being against authentic bowling, but the outcome was a Glamorgan victory as a century from Alan Butcher, supported by fifties from Maynard and Viv Richards, saw the Welsh county romp to a five-wicket win, and all after Warwickshire opener Andy Moles had scored an unbeaten 224 on the opening day of the contest.

Besides some remarkable batting feats, Swansea has also witnessed some exceptional pieces of fielding with perhaps the greatest pick up and throw in Glamorgan's entire history coming at the St. Helen's ground in 1969 with the run-out of the final Essex batsman to secure a last-ball victory which took the Club to the verge of the Championship title. The man responsible was Ossie Wheatley, who had virtually called a halt to his cricket career the previous season when he finished on top of the county's averages with 82 victims at just 12 runs apiece, and being honoured as one of the five Wisden 'Cricketers of the Year'.

As far as 1969 was concerned, Ossie was in semi-retirement yet on the final day of Championship cricket that summer at Swansea he made a key contribution with the vital run out to put his adopted county one victory away from the Championship title. Whilst not being renowned as a fielder *par excellence*, he struck with deadly precision as the visitors needed three off the final delivery to snatch victory and to stifle Glamorgan's title ambitions.

When John Lever played the ball down to third man, he and his tenth-wicket partner Ray East scampered off in pursuit of a last-gasp victory. But it ended in only one run as Wheatley galloped around the boundary in front of the famous Fred's Bar at the Mumbles Road End and returned the ball arrow-like over the stumps and into the gloves of Eifion Jones with the wicketkeeper swiftly doing the rest. Lever was well short of his ground on his way back for a second run. Glamorgan had won by one run and the points acquired put them in a virtually unassailable position at the top of the Championship table.

Eifion had starred in the previous game at Swansea as Glamorgan strengthened their Championship credentials with a thrilling win over Middlesex with Eifion clinching it by hitting the penultimate ball of the match from Ron Hooker for six over long on. As he later reflected

> "It all came down to the last over, with Malcolm Nash and I batting. With two balls to go, I went for the big hit and it came off. I felt it could

The great run out as Eifion Jones whips off the bails as Glamorgan defeat Essex by one run in a thrilling Championship match at Swansea in 1969.

> be our year after that."[6]

As far as the Essex game was concerned, Ossie also had some very fond recollections:

> "I had played only half a dozen games that summer and was just called in from time to time when needs must. I played quite a bit in 1968 but the side were going so well in 1969 and they kept the same side. They didn't really need me.
>
> I had actually retired in 1966 and played only a couple of games in 1967 towards the end of the season. I came back in during 1968 mainly because Jeff Jones broke down. Fortunately, by the Essex match in 1969 I had been playing some club cricket and was in reasonable nick. As the ball made its way towards me I remember thinking whatever I do, it does not have to be particularly quick, but the throw had to be as straight as I could make it. Not having done fielding practice for many years, I managed to wing it in!
>
> There was always a good crowd for our games in August at Swansea and there were a lot of people here that day with many coming onto the field at the end. It was a game that if we won, we were 99 per cent certain of winning the Championship. So the crowd really treated it as 'that's it', and on they came. And St. Helen's was a great place for a celebration, because you just went straight up into the bar!"[7]

1. A.K.Hignell, *Glamorgan 1993-2002: The Glory Years* (Tempus Publishing, 2003).
2. M.P.Maynard with P.Rees, *On the Attack - The Batsman's Story* (Mainstream Publishing, 2001).
3. Ibid.
4. "Reflections by Matthew Maynard" in the Matthew Maynard Testimonial Brochure, 2004.
5. *Western Mail*, 1 July 1977
6. "The Greatest run-out?" by Chris Peregrine, initially published in the *South Wales Evening Post*, and re-printed in the 2010 Glamorgan Yearbook.
7. Ibid.

Chapter Seventeen
A very special place

"A very special place with an almost unique atmosphere of its's own" – the words of a long-standing Glamorgan cricketer when asked to describe the St. Helen's ground in Swansea. During the second half of the 20th century Glamorgan would visit this "special place" up to a dozen times a year for various Championship and limited overs games. Although its share of games in recent times has dropped down to a solitary four-day game plus a one-day match, it is still a popular venue for players, spectators and sponsors.

Some though may disagree, including Micky Norman, the Northamptonshire opening batsman who in a remarkable game at Swansea during mid-June 1964, achieved the rather unenviable distinction of being dismissed first ball twice in the day, and on two occasions had to trudge back up the 90-odd steps from the pavilion doorway down to the edge of the outfield, each time without a run to his name.

It was the clever pace bowling of Ossie Wheatley that proved to be the undoing of the 31 year-old opener, as the Glamorgan captain struck with

The long flight of stairs down to the pitch from the Swansea pavilion, as in 1949 with Wilf Wooller heading out to the middle to bat for Glamorgan.

his first delivery of both innings. The day had begun with Norman fending off a lifter from Wheatley into the hands of Peter Walker at short-leg, and then later in the afternoon, as Northants batted again, he edged the first ball of the second innings from Wheatley straight into the hands of Jim Pressdee in the slips.

As the Glamorgan fielders congratulated their captain for striking again with his opening delivery, the fair-haired Northants batsman had to walk again back up the steps to the Swansea pavilion, not quite believing his ill fortune in having recorded a 'king pair' within the space of six hours of play!

Whilst county games have generally attracted decent crowds at Swansea, it was the match against the touring teams over the August Bank Holiday which were the highlight of the summer calendar at St. Helen's. As Alan Jones recalled when reminiscing about the historic victory over the 1968 Australians:

> "As I travelled into the Swansea ground, it was clear the game had caught the public's imagination. The traffic from the West, from Llanelli, Carmarthen and Gorseinon was far busier than usual. Parking for players at St. Helen's can often be a problem because there is only roadside space available so you have to compete with the spectators. On this particular day, it was obvious we were in for a bumper crowd for I had to walk almost a mile from my parked car."[1]

Right from their earliest days as a first-class county, the well-attended matches against the touring teams at St. Helen's were something of a cash cow for the Club, not least the game at Swansea in August against the 1930 Australians. The game saw the first appearance of Don Bradman at the ground and after a rain-affected first day, the fact that 'The Don' would

The crowd at Swansea in 1930 for the visit of Don Bradman and the Australians.

be continuing his innings on the second day saw long queues outside the ground soon after breakfast time. By the start of play, there were nigh on 25,000 men, women and children people inside St. Helen's, and by the time he had elegantly reached his half-century another couple of thousand had squeezed their way in.

Rain again delayed the start of the final day, and after 21 overs, the Australians set Glamorgan a target of 218 in the remaining 165 minutes. Few gave the Welsh side much of a chance, but to the delight of their supporters, Maurice Turnbull, their young captain and Eddie Bates, the former Yorkshire professional, shared a vibrant stand of 93 in just over an hour. Both men scored attractive fifties as word spread like wildfire around Swansea that Glamorgan might be about to beat Australia. By the time, many hundreds had made their excuses at work and had arrived at St. Helen's, both batsmen had fallen to Clarrie Grimmett, and with the pressure mounting, there was a steady clatter of wickets, as Glamorgan ended 21 runs short with three wickets in hand when the umpires ended what had been a most enjoyable game, and a massive money spinner for the Welsh county.

The huge embankment lining Gorse Lane, as seen in 1973 for the one-day international between England and New Zealand.

These were the days when there was a huge bank lining Gorse Lane, whilst the massive rugby grandstand towered over the outfield at the Mumbles Road End, giving the ground its amphitheatre-like quality. It could be a bit soulless during a club match, but as Johnnie Clay recalled:

> "The place came alive during the fixtures over the touring teams, with the games standing shoulder to shoulder alongside the rugby internationals in the diaries of Welsh sports lovers. In those years either side of the War we twice played the tourists, with the first game at Cardiff over Whitsun often being more like a run-of-the-mill game. The second match, at Swansea in August was something very different in that heady cauldron which is St. Helen's.

A view of the action from Swansea in 1949 when Glamorgan played New Zealand.

> The place would come alive, fuelled by a heady mix of Celtic passion, *hwyl* and a heartfelt desire from the thousands of locals for the home-bred cricketers to do well against the Test players from abroad."[2]

These are thoughts echoed again by Alan Jones who, from an early age had been taken by his father and brothers to watch these matches at the Swansea ground:

> "All my boyhood dreams had been built at St. Helen's... As a teenager, I used to await the arrival of a touring side to St. Helen's with baited breath. This was the chance to see those heroes I had only heard about on radio commentaries."[3]

Richard Bentley, the Swansea-born teacher and author, also fell in love with St. Helen's after visiting the ground for the first time over the August Bank Holiday to watch the game with the 1955 South Africans. At the time, Richard was football-mad with his heroes up the road at the Vetch Field during the 1950s, so as he admits the names of the players on either side meant nothing to him.

> "But in a way, what I do remember is even more precious. I remember the excitement. The sense of occasion. The chatter of the crowd. The applause – in turn passionate and polite. I remember sitting cross-legged and crouched on the grass in front of the double-faced scoreboard. The smell of the new-mown outfield. The run and tickle of grass on my short-trousered knees.
>
> I remember the mix of colours, and especially the bright red ball on the green-ness of the field (so different to the dreary greys of the small

black and white television). I remember warm cheese-and-cucumber sandwiches. And Dandelion and Burdock pop. And melting ice-cream from the van.

I remember the shout of the white-coated scorecard sellers. The newly printed card. The responsibility of entering the wickets (in best writing, of course). I remember the crack of ball on bat. The pounding feet of the boundary fielder. The speed of the ball. In short, I remember falling in love with cricket - and with St. Helen's."[4]

A view of the ecstatic crowd after Glamorgan's victory over the 1968 Australians.

Richard's heartfelt recollections were initially published in a special booklet published to celebrate the 40th anniversary of the St. Helen's Balconiers, the Swansea-based supporters organisation who have done so much in recent years to preserve county cricket at this West Walian outpost and at a time when other out-grounds and festival weeks have been erased from the cricketing calendar.

Their name stems from the popular area of seating on the balcony of the old Swansea pavilion, and it was here that the great and the good of Swansea's cricketing world would watch the county games. In 1972 Roy Fredericks and Alan Jones - whose Benefit Year it was - delighted those on the balcony by sharing what was then Glamorgan's best-ever opening stand in first-class cricket, adding 330 for the first wicket against Northamptonshire. When Alan was dismissed, one of the cognoscenti, Danny Lewis, remarked, "This is the sort of occasion on which a collection

The old two-sided scoreboard at Swansea, recording the record partnership in 1972 by the Glamorgan openers against Northamptonshire.

Roy Fredericks and Alan Jones walk out to the middle to continue their record-breaking stand at Swansea in 1972.

should be made for a player in his Benefit Year." Richard Bentley takes up the story:

> "An approach was duly made to Wilf Wooller, the Club Secretary, who replied that unfortunately it was not possible as only a certain number of collections are allowed by set rule and Alan Jones' allocation had already been used. Danny Lewis then enquired whether collections other than official might be made. 'Certainly' replied Mr. Wooller 'I'll make an announcement and arrange for the buckets.' The friends who sat together with Danny - Gwyn Rees, David Evans, Gerald Munday and Owen Pughe made the collection. The crowd was sparse, being a Monday, but the sum of £109 was collected. They were delighted - the Society was formed."[5]

In the intervening years, the Balconiers, through the tireless work of committee member John Williams, have held Annual Awards evenings as well as running coach trips to Cardiff and a host of county grounds the length and breadth of England so that Glamorgan supporters could follow their county team. Sponsorship of other events and players have followed, besides raising in excess of £350,000 since their founding in 1972 to ensure that a festival of county cricket takes place each year in Swansea.

To some, the annual festival at St. Helen's is an anachronism, especially given the other changes to the sporting landscape in the former Copperopolis, now dominated by a modern stadium, a Premier League football team and a regional rugby side. In 2003, in what many diehard supporters of the All

Welsh rugby international Phil Bennett makes a special presentation on behalf of the St. Helen's Balconiers in front of the Swansea pavilion to Glamorgan's Arthur Francis after a one-day game in 1975.

Whites thought could never happen, Neath RFC and Swansea RFC merged as the Ospreys came into being. The advent of regional rugby being staged at the Liberty Stadium, means that top-class rugby no longer takes place at St. Helen's, with the massive wooden grandstand having been demolished and replaced by a smaller metallic structure.

A mile or so to the east of St. Helen's, the Vetch Field – the home of Swansea City FC - was demolished during 2011. The diggers and bulldozers moved in just a few months short of the ground's centenary, with the final Football League fixture having been staged at the Vetch during the last week of April 2005. Much of the area is now used for allotments whilst Swansea Corporation have also earmarked St. Helen's – the last bastion of Victorian and Edwardian sport in the city – as a potential area for house-building.

Despite dark clouds hanging over the long-term future of St. Helen's both as a county cricket ground and as a sporting venue, John Williams and his loyal band of supporters in the Balconiers continue to organise Glamorgan matches at the Swansea venue and, at what, they still consider "a very special place."

John Williams in front of one of the coaches taking the Balconiers and other Glamorgan supporters to away grounds.

1. A.Jones with T.Stevens, *Hooked on Opening* (Gomer Publishing, 1984).
2. Comments by Johnnie Clay in a script for a BBC Wales radio programme on Glamorgan cricket circa 1960.
3. A. Jones op. cit.
4. R.Bentley, *St. Helen's - an atmosphere of its own,* (St. Helen's Balconiers, 2012).
5. The Balconiers Newsletter, Number 1 in St. Helen's, as quoted in St.Heln's - an atmosphere of its own" op.cit.

Appendix A

Glamorgan's First-Class Matches played at St Helen's, Swansea

28th May 1921	County Championship	v Leicestershire
1st June 1921	County Championship	v Gloucestershire
15th June 1921	County Championship	v Somerset
27th July 1921	County Championship	v Worcestershire
30th July 1921	Tourist Match	v Australians
17th May 1922	County Championship	v Sussex
20th May 1922	County Championship	v Hampshire
7th June 1922	County Championship	v Northamptonshire
14th June 1922	County Championship	v Derbyshire
22nd July 1922	County Championship	v Lancashire
2nd June 1923	County Championship	v Northamptonshire
30th June 1923	County Championship	v Nottinghamshire
28th July 1923	County Championship	v Leicestershire
1st August 1923	County Championship	v Gloucestershire
24th May 1924	County Championship	v Surrey
28th May 1924	County Championship	v Leicestershire
5th July 1924	County Championship	v Worcestershire
12th July 1924	County Championship	v Derbyshire
13th August 1924	County Championship	v Lancashire
27th August 1924	First-Class Friendly	v HDG Leveson-Gower's XI
10th June 1925	County Championship	v Lancashire
27th June 1925	County Championship	v Gloucestershire
11th July 1925	County Championship	v Essex
25th July 1925	County Championship	v Northamptonshire
1st August 1925	First-Class Friendly	v HDG Leveson-Gower's XI
26th August 1925	County Championship	v Warwickshire
29th August 1925	County Championship	v Nottinghamshire
30th June 1926	County Championship	v Nottinghamshire
14th July 1926	County Championship	v Warwickshire
28th July 1926	County Championship	v Leicestershire
31st July 1926	Tourist Match	v Australians
18th August 1926	County Championship	v Gloucestershire
28th August 1926	County Championship	v Yorkshire
25th May 1927	County Championship	v Lancashire
11th June 1927	County Championship	v Derbyshire
13th July 1927	County Championship	v Warwickshire
6th August 1927	County Championship	v Essex
10th August 1927	County Championship	v Surrey
31st August 1927	County Championship	v Nottinghamshire
9th June 1928	County Championship	v Lancashire
7th July 1928	County Championship	v Sussex
4th August 1928	Tourist Match	v West Indians
15th August 1928	County Championship	v Essex
18th August 1928	County Championship	v Northamptonshire
29th August 1928	County Championship	v Yorkshire
22nd May 1929	County Championship	v Hampshire
1st June 1929	County Championship	v Lancashire
26th June 1929	County Championship	v Gloucestershire
24th July 1929	County Championship	v Worcestershire
3rd August 1929	Tourist Match	v South Africans
17th August 1929	County Championship	v Sussex
31st August 1929	County Championship	v Northamptonshire
14th May 1930	County Championship	v Surrey

4th June 1930	County Championship	v Derbyshire
28th June 1930	County Championship	v Warwickshire
12th July 1930	County Championship	v Yorkshire
2nd August 1930	Tourist Match	v Australians
20th August 1930	County Championship	v Essex
27th August 1930	County Championship	v Gloucestershire
20th May 1931	County Championship	v Lancashire
27th May 1931	County Championship	v Hampshire
20th June 1931	County Championship	v Warwickshire
15th July 1931	County Championship	v Middlesex
22nd July 1931	County Championship	v Yorkshire
1st August 1931	Tourist Match	v New Zealanders
29th August 1931	First-Class Friendly	v Nottinghamshire
28th May 1932	County Championship	v Surrey
4th June 1932	County Championship	v Kent
22nd June 1932	County Championship	v Gloucestershire
16th July 1932	County Championship	v Northamptonshire
20th July 1932	County Championship	v Worcestershire
30th July 1932	Tourist Match	v Indians
10th August 1932	County Championship	v Sussex
27th May 1933	County Championship	v Essex
10th June 1933	County Championship	v Northamptonshire
21st June 1933	County Championship	v Lancashire
5th July 1933	County Championship	v Nottinghamshire
12th July 1933	County Championship	v Middlesex
5th August 1933	Tourist Match	v West Indians
16th May 1934	County Championship	v Yorkshire
26th May 1934	County Championship	v Leicestershire
20th June 1934	County Championship	v Warwickshire
21st July 1934	County Championship	v Somerset
4th August 1934	Tourist Match	v Australians
22nd May 1935	County Championship	v Worcestershire
15th June 1935	County Championship	v Nottinghamshire
10th July 1935	County Championship	v Warwickshire
24th July 1935	County Championship	v Lancashire
3rd August 1935	Tourist Match	v South Africans
13th May 1936	County Championship	v Sussex
20th May 1936	County Championship	v Yorkshire
6th June 1936	County Championship	v Hampshire
11th July 1936	County Championship	v Leicestershire
1st August 1936	Tourist Match	v Indians
1st May 1937	County Championship	v Kent
2nd June 1937	County Championship	v Hampshire
23rd June 1937	County Championship	v Worcestershire
10th July 1937	County Championship	v Northamptonshire
31st July 1937	Tourist Match	v New Zealanders
28th May 1938	County Championship	v Essex
18th June 1938	University Match	v Cambridge University
29th June 1938	County Championship	v Sussex
30th July 1938	Tourist Match	v Australians
17th August 1938	County Championship	v Lancashire
3rd June 1939	County Championship	v Nottinghamshire
5th July 1939	County Championship	v Hampshire
26th July 1939	County Championship	v Leicestershire
5th August 1939	Tourist Match	v West Indians
23rd August 1939	County Championship	v Surrey
25th May 1946	County Championship	v Northamptonshire
19th June 1946	County Championship	v Middlesex
10th July 1946	County Championship	v Hampshire
3rd August 1946	Tourist Match	v Indians
10th May 1947	County Championship	v Yorkshire
4th June 1947	County Championship	v Derbyshire
14th June 1947	County Championship	v Gloucestershire

2nd July 1947	County Championship	v Warwickshire
2nd August 1947	Tourist Match	v South Africans
13th August 1947	County Championship	v Northamptonshire
22nd May 1948	County Championship	v Somerset
12th June 1948	County Championship	v Kent
23rd June 1948	County Championship	v Nottinghamshire
7th July 1948	County Championship	v Sussex
31st July 1948	Australia in British Isles	v Australians
15th September 1948	First-Class Friendly	v South of England
14th May 1949	County Championship	v Warwickshire
1st June 1949	County Championship	v Middlesex
18th June 1949	County Championship	v Kent
30th July 1949	Tourist Match	v New Zealanders
24th August 1949	County Championship	v Leicestershire
6th May 1950	County Championship	v Nottinghamshire
17th June 1950	County Championship	v Surrey
19th July 1950	County Championship	v Lancashire
5th August 1950	Tourist Match	v West Indians
9th August 1950	County Championship	v Hampshire
26th August 1950	County Championship	v Warwickshire
9th May 1951	County Championship	v Warwickshire
6th June 1951	County Championship	v Northamptonshire
4th July 1951	County Championship	v Kent
1st August 1951	County Championship	v Middlesex
4th August 1951	Tourist Match	v South Africans
25th August 1951	County Championship	v Gloucestershire
24th May 1952	County Championship	v Somerset
4th June 1952	County Championship	v Yorkshire
28th June 1952	County Championship	v Derbyshire
16th July 1952	County Championship	v Hampshire
2nd August 1952	Tourist Match	v Indians
23rd August 1952	County Championship	v Sussex
9th May 1953	County Championship	v Worcestershire
20th June 1953	County Championship	v Somerset
18th July 1953	County Championship	v Gloucestershire
1st August 1953	Tourist Match	v Australians
19th August 1953	County Championship	v Lancashire
19th May 1954	County Championship	v Lancashire
29th May 1954	County Championship	v Leicestershire
16th June 1954	County Championship	v Middlesex
10th July 1954	County Championship	v Kent
31st July 1954	Tourist Match	v Pakistanis
14th August 1954	County Championship	v Sussex
14th May 1955	County Championship	v Lancashire
11th June 1955	County Championship	v Gloucestershire
25th June 1955	County Championship	v Hampshire
20th July 1955	County Championship	v Surrey
30th July 1955	Tourist Match	v South Africans
3rd August 1955	County Championship	v Worcestershire
23rd May 1956	County Championship	v Kent
9th June 1956	County Championship	v Derbyshire
23rd June 1956	County Championship	v Worcestershire
18th July 1956	County Championship	v Yorkshire
4th August 1956	Tourist Match	v Australians
25th May 1957	County Championship	v Sussex
12th June 1957	County Championship	v Somerset
29th June 1957	County Championship	v Gloucestershire
17th July 1957	County Championship	v Hampshire
3rd August 1957	Tourist Match	v West Indians
24th August 1957	County Championship	v Middlesex
28th May 1958	County Championship	v Kent
7th June 1958	County Championship	v Warwickshire
28th June 1958	County Championship	v Derbyshire

9th July 1958	County Championship	v Surrey
2nd August 1958	Tourist Match	v New Zealanders
23rd August 1958	County Championship	v Yorkshire
13th May 1959	County Championship	v Worcestershire
27th May 1959	County Championship	v Derbyshire
13th June 1959	County Championship	v Gloucestershire
4th July 1959	County Championship	v Middlesex
1st August 1959	Tourist Match	v Indians
15th August 1959	County Championship	v Somerset
7th May 1960	County Championship	v Leicestershire
28th May 1960	County Championship	v Hampshire
8th June 1960	County Championship	v Warwickshire
9th July 1960	County Championship	v Nottinghamshire
30th July 1960	Tourist Match	v South Africans
17th August 1960	County Championship	v Yorkshire
13th May 1961	County Championship	v Yorkshire
3rd June 1961	County Championship	v Hampshire
28th June 1961	County Championship	v Warwickshire
8th July 1961	County Championship	v Kent
5th August 1961	Tourist Match	v Australians
23rd August 1961	County Championship	v Northamptonshire
16th May 1962	County Championship	v Nottinghamshire
26th May 1962	County Championship	v Warwickshire
23rd June 1962	County Championship	v Somerset
21st July 1962	County Championship	v Northamptonshire
4th August 1962	Tourist Match	v Pakistanis
18th August 1962	County Championship	v Derbyshire
11th May 1963	County Championship	v Hampshire
25th May 1963	County Championship	v Derbyshire
5th June 1963	County Championship	v Essex
8th June 1963	County Championship	v Surrey
3rd July 1963	County Championship	v Worcestershire
3rd August 1963	Tourist Match	v West Indians
28th August 1963	County Championship	v Lancashire
23rd May 1964	County Championship	v Essex
10th June 1964	County Championship	v Northamptonshire
8th July 1964	County Championship	v Yorkshire
11th July 1964	County Championship	v Somerset
1st August 1964	Tourist Match	v Australians
15th August 1964	County Championship	v Nottinghamshire
29th May 1965	County Championship	v Kent
9th June 1965	County Championship	v Yorkshire
30th June 1965	County Championship	v Middlesex
3rd July 1965	County Championship	v Lancashire
21st July 1965	County Championship	v Hampshre
31st July 1965	Tourist Match	v South Africans
28th August 1965	County Championship	v Surrey
25th May 1966	County Championship	v Warwickshire
8th June 1966	County Championship	v Leicestershire
25th June 1966	County Championship	v Nottinghamshire
13th July 1966	County Championship	v Sussex
27th July 1966	County Championship	v Essex
30th July 1966	Tourist Match	v West Indians
27th May 1967	County Championship	v Hampshire
10th June 1967	County Championship	v Yorkshire
21st June 1967	County Championship	v Sussex
22nd July 1967	County Championship	v Middlesex
5th August 1967	Tourist Match	v Pakistanis
9th August 1967	County Championship	v Warwickshire
22nd May 1968	County Championship	v Worcestershire
15th June 1968	County Championship	v Northamptonshire
29th June 1968	County Championship	v Kent
17th July 1968	County Championship	v Somerset

3rd August 1968	Tourist Match	v Australians
31st August 1968	County Championship	v Nottinghamshire
3rd May 1969	County Championship	v Yorkshire
1th June 1969	County Championship	v Lancashire
5th July 1969	Tourist Match	v West Indians
26th July 1969	County Championship	v Warwickshire
20th August 1969	County Championship	v Middlesex
30th August 1969	County Championship	v Essex
2nd May 1970	County Championship	v Kent
3rd June 1970	County Championship	v Somerset
4th July 1970	County Championship	v Gloucestershire
25th July 1970	Tourist Match	v Jamaica
19th August 1970	County Championship	v Sussex
29th August 1970	County Championship	v Derbyshire
22nd May 1971	County Championship	v Lancashire
5th June 1971	County Championship	v Hampshire
23rd June 1971	Tourist Match	v Pakistanis
24th July 1971	County Championship	v Northamptonshire
4th August 1971	County Championship	v Nottinghamshire
7th August 1971	County Championship	v Yorkshire
27th May 1972	Tourist Match	v Australians
10th June 1972	County Championship	v Somerset
28th June 1972	First-class Friendly	v Cambridge University
1st July 1972	County Championship	v Gloucestershire
12th August 1972	County Championship	v Essex
26th August 1972	County Championship	v Northamptonshire
26th May 1973	County Championship	v Hampshire
23rd June 1973	County Championship	v Lancashire
7th July 1973	Tourist Match	v West Indians
28th July 1973	County Championship	v Kent
18th August 1973	County Championship	v Gloucestershire
8th June 1974	County Championship	v Gloucestershire
15th June 1974	County Championship	v Northamptonshire
27th July 1974	County Championship	v Somerset
3rd August 1974	Tourist Match	v Pakistanis
21st August 1974	County Championship	v Essex
14th May 1975	County Championship	v Hampshire
7th June 1975	County Championship	v Warwickshire
18th June 1975	County Championship	v Kent
2nd July 1975	First-class friendly	v Cambridge University
5th July 1975	Tourist Match	v Australians
26th July 1975	County Championship	v Lancashire
23rd August 1975	County Championship	v Worcestershire
19th May 1976	County Championship	v Essex
29th May 1976	County Championship	v Leicestershire
3rd July 1976	County Championship	v Nottinghamshire
7th August 1976	Tourist Match	v West Indians
14th August 1976	County Championship	v Middlesex
11th May 1977	County Championship	v Derbyshire
14th May 1977	Australia in British Isles	v Australians
11th June 1977	County Championship	v Warwickshire
29th June 1977	County Championship	v Worcestershire
30th July 1977	County Championship	v Kent
27th August 1977	County Championship	v Lancashire
27th May 1978	County Championship	v Hampshire
3rd June 1978	County Championship	v Leicestershire
5th July 1978	Tourist Match	v New Zealanders
15th July 1978	County Championship	v Middlesex
12th August 1978	County Championship	v Nottinghamshire
23rd August 1978	County Championship	v Sussex
9th May 1979	County Championship	v Worcestershire
9th June 1979	County Championship	v Warwickshire
7th July 1979	County Championship	v Somerset

Date	Match	Opponent
14th July 1979	Tourist Match	v Sri Lankans
25th July 1979	Tourist Match	v Indians
28th July 1979	County Championship	v Lancashire
25th August 1979	County Championship	v Derbyshire
30th April 1980	County Championship	v Essex
24th May 1980	County Championship	v Nottinghamshire
14th June 1980	County Championship	v Worcestershire
28th June 1980	Tourist Match	v West Indians
9th July 1980	County Championship	v Sussex
16th August 1980	County Championship	v Gloucestershire
27th May 1981	Tourist Match	v Australians
6th June 1981	County Championship	v Surrey
27th June 1981	County Championship	v Somerset
1st July 1981	County Championship	v Hampshire
15th August 1981	County Championship	v Derbyshire
26th August 1981	County Championship	v Worcestershire
29th May 1982	County Championship	v Gloucestershire
2nd June 1982	County Championship	v Somerset
9th June 1982	County Championship	v Middlesex
19th June 1982	First-class Friendly	v Oxford University
3rd July 1982	Tourist Match	v Pakistanis
7th August 1982	County Championship	v Northamptonshire
21st August 1982	County Championship	v Nottinghamshire
28th May 1983	County Championship	v Gloucestershire
15th June 1983	County Championship	v Somerset
13th July 1983	County Championship	v Lancashire
30th July 1983	County Championship	v Surrey
20th August 1983	County Championship	v Derbyshire
26th May 1984	Tourist Match	v West Indians
2nd June 1984	County Championship	v Worcestershire
27th June 1984	County Championship	v Middlesex
30th June 1984	County Championship	v Leicestershire
28th July 1984	County Championship	v Derbyshire
18th August 1984	County Championship	v Northamptonshire
29th August 1984	County Championship	v Surrey
15th June 1985	County Championship	v Essex
19th June 1985	Tourist Match	v Zimbabweans
6th July 1985	County Championship	v Nottinghamshire
10th July 1985	County Championship	v Leicestershire
3rd August 1985	County Championship	v Kent
24th August 1985	County Championship	v Yorkshire
4th June 1986	County Championship	v Essex
18th June 1986	County Championship	v Warwickshire
21st June 1986	County Championship	v Lancashire
19th July 1986	County Championship	v Northamptonshire
16th August 1986	Tourist Match	v New Zealanders
27th August 1986	County Championship	v Surrey
6th May 1987	County Championship	v Lancashire
3rd June 1987	County Championship	v Hampshire
6th June 1987	County Championship	v Somerset
1st July 1987	County Championship	v Northamptonshire
4th July 1987	County Championship	v Gloucestershire
21st May 1988	County Championship	v Derbyshire
28th May 1988	County Championship	v Gloucestershire
25th June 1988	County Championship	v Lancashire
13th July 1988	Tourist Match	v West Indians
6th August 1988	County Championship	v Surrey
20th May 1989	County Championship	v Northamptonshire
8th July 1989	County Championship	v Essex
12th August 1989	County Championship	v Sussex
24th August 1989	County Championship	v Warwickshire
23rd May 1990	County Championship	v Kent
4th July 1990	County Championship	v Gloucestershire

25th July 1990	County Championship	v Warwickshire
18th August 1990	Tourist Match	v Indians
16th May 1991	County Championship	v Warwickshire
4th June 1991	County Championship	v Somerset
16th July 1991	Tourist Match	v West Indians
9th August 1991	County Championship	v Hampshire
20th May 1992	County Championship	v Warwickshire
29th May 1992	County Championship	v Leicestershire
31st July 1992	County Championship	v Kent
21st August 1992	County Championship	v Gloucestershire
20th May 1993	County Championship	v Northamptonshire
24th June 1993	County Championship	v Nottinghamshire
19th August 1993	County Championship	v Hampshire
2nd June 1994	County Championship	v Surrey
8th June 1994	Tourist Match	v New Zealanders
28th July 1994	County Championship	v Somerset
11th May 1995	County Championship	v Sussex
29th June 1995	County Championship	v Durham
10th August 1995	County Championship	v Essex
13th June 1996	County Championship	v Somerset
8th August 1996	County Championship	v Leicestershire
26th June 1997	County Championship	v Sussex
2nd July 1997	County Championship	v Gloucestershire
1st July 1998	County Championship	v Surrey
30th June 1999	County Championship	v Hampshire
28th June 2000	County Championship	v Worcestershire
25th May 2001	County Championship	v Kent
30th May 2001	County Championship	v Yorkshire
3rd July 2002	County Championship	v Essex
4th June 2003	County Championship	v Derbyshire
24th July 2003	Tourist Match	v India A
2nd June 2004	County Championship	v Somerset
21st July 2004	Tourist Match	v Sri Lanka A
1st June 2005	County Championship	v Sussex
31st May 2006	County Championship	v Somerset
20th June 2006	County Championship	v Surrey
23rd May 2007	County Championship	v Middlesex
30th May 2007	County Championship	v Essex
5th June 2007	County Championship	v Nottinghamshire
21st May 2008	County Championship	v Northamptonshire
20th August 2009	County Championship	v Middlesex
21st July 2010	County Championship	v Leicestershire
27th July 2011	County Championship	v Northamptonshire
1st August 2012	County Championship	v Gloucestershire
21st August 2013	County Championship	v Leicestershire
15th August 2014	County Championship	v Essex
6th August 2015	County Championship	v Gloucestershire
3rd August 2016	County Championship	v Northamptonshire
26th May 2017	County Championship	v Durham
20th June 2018	County Championship	v Derbyshire

Appendix B

Glamorgan's List A Matches played at St Helen's, Swansea

21st May 1966	Gillette Cup	v Warwickshire
18th May 1969	Player's County League	v Hampshire
7th June 1969	Gillette Cup	v Hertfordshire
27th July 1969	Player's County League	v Warwickshire
31st August 1969	Player's County League	v Essex
3rd May 1970	John Player League	v Kent
30th May 1970	Gillette Cup	v Surrey
30th August 1970	John Player League	v Derbyshire
30th May 1971	John Player League	v Warwickshire
8th August 1971	John Player League	v Yorkshire
29th April 1972	Benson and Hedges Cup	v Gloucestershire
14th May 1972	John Player League	v Yorkshire
11th June 1972	John Player League	v Warwickshire
27th August 1972	John Player League	v Surrey
12th May 1973	Benson and Hedges Cup	v Hampshire
2nd June 1973	Benson and Hedges Cup	v Minor Counties South
24th June 1973	John Player League	v Lancashire
8th July 1973	Tourist Match	v West Indians
29th July 1973	John Player League	v Kent
2nd September 1973	John Player League	v Middlesex
27th April 1974	Benson and Hedges Cup	v Somerset
16th June 1974	John Player League	v Northamptonshire
29th June 1974	Gillette Cup	v Lincolnshire
7th July 1974	John Player League	v Nottinghamshire
28th July 1974	John Player League	v Somerset
11th May 1975	John Player League	v Surrey
21st May 1975	Benson and Hedges Cup	v Hampshire
8th June 1975	John Player League	v Warwickshire
27th July 1975	John Player League	v Lancashire
8th May 1976	Benson and Hedges Cup	v Hampshire
30th May 1976	John Player League	v Leicestershire
4th July 1976	John Player League	v Nottinghamshire
8th August 1976	Tourist Match	v West Indians
15th August 1976	John Player League 1976	v Derbyshire
7th May 1977	Benson and Hedges Cup	v Worcestershire
8th June 1977	Benson and Hedges Cup	v Hampshire
12th June 1977	John Player League 1977	v Warwickshire
17th July 1977	John Player League 1977	v Kent
17th August 1977	Gillette Cup	v Leicestershire
28th August 1977	John Player League	v Lancashire
6th May 1978	Benson and Hedges Cup	v Hampshire
28th May 1978	John Player League	v Hampshire
4th June 1978	John Player League	v Leicestershire
16th July 1978	John Player League	v Middlesex
13th August 1978	John Player League	v Nottinghamshire
13th May 1979	John Player League	v Sussex
19th May 1979	Benson and Hedges Cup	v Gloucestershire
10th June 1979	John Player League	v Warwickshire
27th June 1979	Gillette Cup	v Kent
8th July 1979	John Player League	v Somerset
26th August 1979	John Player League	v Derbyshire
17th May 1980	Benson and Hedges Cup	v Minor Counties
18th May 1980	John Player League	v Essex

25th May 1980	John Player League	v Nottinghamshire
15th June 1980	John Player League	v Yorkshire
29th June 1980	Tourist Match	v West Indians
17th August 1980	John Player League	v Gloucestershire
9th May 1981	Benson and Hedges Cup	v Essex
7th June 1981	John Player League	v Surrey
28th June 1981	John Player League	v Warwickshire
16th August 1981	John Player League	v Derbyshire
25th May 1982	Benson and Hedges Cup	v Somerset
30th May 1982	John Player League	v Somerset
4th July 1982	Tourist Match	v Pakistanis
25th July 1982	John Player League	v Middlesex
22nd August 1982	John Player League	v Nottinghamshire
15th May 1983	John Player Special League	v Warwickshire
21st May 1983	Benson and Hedges Cup	v Kent
23rd May 1983	Benson and Hedges Cup	v Kent
29th May 1983	John Player Special League	v Lancashire
20th July 1983	Nat West Bank Trophy	v Hampshire
31st July 1983	John Player Special League	v Surrey
21st August 1983	John Player Special League	v Derbyshire
5th May 1984	Benson and Hedges Cup	v Somerset
6th May 1984	John Player Special League	v Gloucestershire
1st July 1984	John Player Special League	v Leicestershire
4th July 1984	Nat West Bank Trophy	v Nottinghamshire
19th August 1984	John Player Special League	v Northamptonshire
11th May 1985	Benson and Hedges Cup	v Minor Counties
16th June 1985	John Player Special League	v Essex
7th July 1985	John Player Special League	v Nottinghamshire
7th August 1985	Nat West Bank Trophy	v Worcestershire
25th August 1985	John Player Special League	v Yorkshire
10th May 1986	Benson and Hedges Cup	v Sussex
11th May 1986	John Player Special League	v Leicestershire
17th May 1986	Benson and Hedges Cup	v Gloucestershire
22nd June 1986	John Player Special League	v Lancashire
4th May 1987	Benson and Hedges Cup	v Sussex
17th May 1987	Refuge Assurance League	v Kent
26th July 1987	Refuge Assurance League	v Warwickshire
16th August 1987	Refuge Assurance League	v Worcestershire
14th May 1988	Benson and Hedges Cup	v Gloucestershire
8th June 1988	Benson and Hedges Cup	v Derbyshire
14th August 1988	Refuge Assurance League	v Worcestershire
13th May 1989	Benson and Hedges Cup	v Sussex
30th July 1989	Refuge Assurance League	v Hampshire
12th May 1990	Benson and Hedges Cup	v Kent
27th June 1990	Nat West Bank Trophy	v Dorset
29th July 1990	Refuge Assurance League	v Derbyshire
26th August 1990	Refuge Assurance League	v Worcestershire
19th May 1991	Refuge Assurance League	v Warwickshire
26th May 1991	Refuge Assurance League	v Sussex
4th August 1991	Refuge Assurance League	v Gloucestershire
31st May 1992	Sunday League	v Leicestershire
24th June 1992	Nat West Bank Trophy	v Surrey
29th July 1992	Nat West Bank Trophy	v Northamptonshire
2nd August 1992	Sunday League	v Kent
22nd June 1993	Nat West Bank Trophy	v Oxfordshire
27th June 1993	AXA Equity and Law League	v Nottinghamshire
28th July 1993	Nat West Bank Trophy	v Worcestershire
22nd August 1993	AXA Equity and Law League	v Hampshire
5th June 1994	AXA Equity and Law League	v Surrey
19th June 1994	AXA Equity and Law League	v Derbyshire
21st June 1994	Nat West Bank Trophy	v Lincolnshire
26th July 1994	Nat West Bank Trophy	v Surrey
31st July 1994	AXA Equity and Law League	v Somerset

14th May 1995	AXA Equity and Law League	v Sussex
16th May 1995	Benson and Hedges Cup	v Gloucestershire
2nd July 1995	AXA Equity and Law League	v Durham
16th June 1996	AXA Equity and Law League	v Somerset
28th July 1996	AXA Equity and Law League	v Lancashire
11th August 1996	AXA Equity and Law League	v Leicestershire
29th June 1997	AXA Life League	v Sussex
6th July 1997	AXA Life League	v Gloucestershire
5th July 1998	AXA League	v Surrey
4th July 1999	National League	v Sussex
2nd July 2000	National League	v Warwickshire
3rd June 2001	National League	v Sussex
7th July 2002	National League	v Leicestershire
8th June 2003	National League	v Worcestershire
6th June 2004	totesport League	v Gloucestershire
5th June 2005	totesport League	v Nottinghamshire
4th June 2006	C & G Trophy	v Somerset
27th May 2007	Friends Provident Trophy	v Essex
3rd June 2007	Friends Provident Trophy	v Hampshire
25th May 2008	Friends Provident Trophy	v Worcestershire
19th May 2009	Friends Provident Trophy	v Northamptonshire
25th July 2010	Clydesdale Bank 40	v Sussex
31st July 2011	Clydesdale Bank 40	v Nottinghamshire
5th August 2012	Clydesdale Bank 40	v Nottinghamshire
25th August 2013	Yorkshire Bank 40	v Leicestershire
14th August 2014	Royal London One-Day Cup	v Warwickshire
5th August 2015	Royal London One-Day Cup	v Sussex
31st July 2016	Royal London One-Day Cup	v Hampshire
14th May 2017	Royal London One-Day Cup	v Kent
3rd June 2018	Royal London One-Day Cup	v Hampshire

Glamorgan's Twenty20 matches at St. Helen's, Swansea

25th June 2005	Twenty20 Cup	v Warwickshire

Appendix C
Dedication

This book is dedicated to the memory of sports writer, historian and cricket lover Bob Harragan, as well as two other gentlemen, Harvey Thomas and Alcwyn Jenkins, both of whom tragically lost their lives as a result of cricketing activities at St. Helen's.

Harvey Thomas was a building contractor and property developer who, during the 1900s enthusiastically played cricket for Swansea's 3rd XI, as well as making occasional appearances for the club's 2nd XI and Wednesday afternoon team. He embodied the type of sportsmen for whom St. Helen's existed purely in terms of recreational cricket and healthy exercise. Harvey harboured no ambitions for appearing for the Swansea 1st XI, nor the county side - instead it was playing, practicing and socialising with his friends in the club which meant most to him.

Sadly, it was also to cost Harvey his life as on 13 June 1907, the thirty year-old was struck on the head whilst bowling in the nets at St. Helen's.[1] A fortnight before he had also been hit on the head whilst playing for Swansea 3rd XI at Ammanford, with his nasty head wound requiring a couple of stitches. He soon recovered and on that fateful afternoon in June 1907, he was bowling in the nets at St. Helen's to Jack Bancroft, the 1st XI wicket-keeper, together with Billy Trew – the captain of the Swansea 1st XV - and George Davies.[2]

The tragic accident happened after Trew had bowled a short ball to Bancroft which was forcibly struck towards mid-off where Davies and Thomas were standing and awaiting their turn to bowl. Sensing what could happen, Bancroft shouted out, with Davies ducking but Thomas turned and was struck on his neck below his left ear. Thomas fell to the ground and was helped to his nearby home. He went straight to bed but two days later he fell unconscious and passed away shortly afterwards.

On 4 July 2009 Alcwyn Jenkins, a well-liked umpire, was killed whilst standing in the South Wales Cricket Association match between Swansea and Llangennech at St. Helen's.[3] Alcwyn had stood for over 25 years both senior and junior cricket, besides officiating in several 2nd XI matches for Glamorgan as well as accompanying various representative teams from South Wales on their overseas tours.

His tragic death came shortly after an interruption to the League match because of rain as he was struck on the side of the head by a ball thrown in by a fielder from the boundary. Efforts were made to resuscitate the 72-year old before the air ambulance was called to carry him to hospital. According to one spectator "It was a freak accident, and no one was to blame. The fielder threw the ball back to the wicket from about forty yards away — it happens dozens of times in a game. But the umpire didn't see it coming."

Neil Hobbs, Honorary Chairman of the South Wales Cricket Association, said: "No one can quite believe it has happened. Umpires do get hit by the ball occasionally, but the chances of it being a fatality must be less than one in a million." The match was duly abandoned and the following weekend a minute's silence was held at all League games in South Wales as a mark of respect for one of the League's most popular umpires. A minute's silence also took place before play on the second day of the 2009 Ashes Test Match at Cardiff as England met Australia in the opening match of the iconic series.

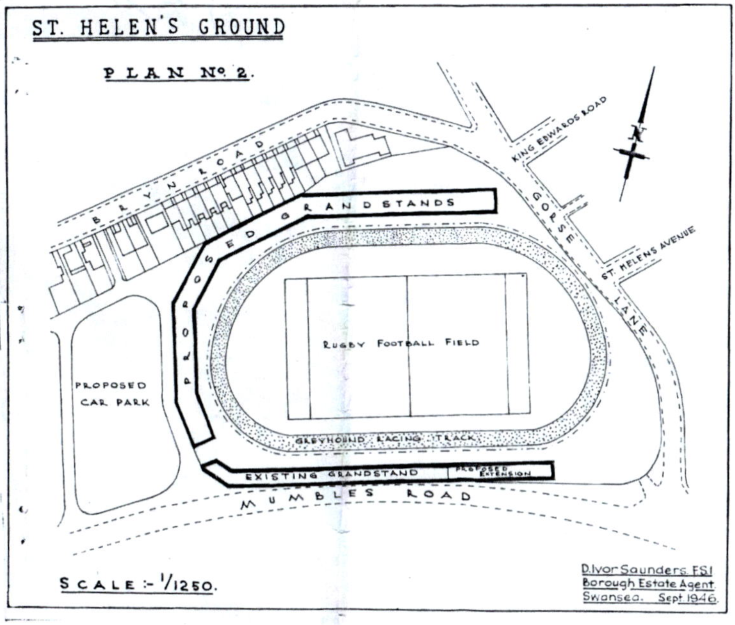

St. Helen's could have been more of a sporting amphitheatre had the plans above for additional grandstands, dated September 1946, been given the green light. Given the scale of re-building after wartime bombing, elsewhere in Swansea, the Corporation dropped these plans.

1 *Evening Express*, 18 June 1907.

2 Billy Trew appeared on 29 occasions for the Welsh rugby team and also led Swansea RFC to their victories over Australia and South Africa in 1908 and 1912 respectively.

3 Glamorgan Yearbook 2010.

Acknowledgements

Bob Harragan had completed a chapter-by-chapter synopsis, plus a rough draft of half a dozen chapters by the time his health deteriorated and I'm very grateful to his brother John for extracting Bob's efforts, plus his working notes on the remaining sections. From telephone conversations and emails with Bob, I had a good idea of how he envisaged the finished work so I hope that I have done him justice in finishing things off and filling in the gaps from his rough drafts.

Thanks also to John Williams of the St. Helen's Balconiers for access to a number of superb images, plus several lengthy chats about his memories of watching and supporting Glamorgan at St. Helen's since the 1960s. My thanks also to Richard Bentley for his recollections of county cricket at Swansea, plus the whereabouts of some of the quoted material, and also to Edward Cooper, another staunch Glamorgan supporter, who kindly helped with the photography, including the outstanding image which adorns the front cover and captures the unique, maritime atmosphere of the ground.

A group of local historians and sporting experts also kindly assisted with the early days of cricket and rugby in Swansea, including Dave Dow, Gerald Gabb, David Farmer, Peter Stead and Alun Wyn Bevan, whilst my thanks to Felicity Kilpatrick, Jeff Towns and Daryl Leeworthy for other historical nuggets. Over the years, a host of other people, including former players, journalists and Glamorgan supporters, have shared their memories as well as images, and my thanks to them (as listed in alphabetical order): Edward Bevan, the late Ernie Billings, Dave Brayley, Stephen Chalke, Robert Croft, Tony Davies, Peter Davies, the late Bill Edwards, the late Ron Griffiths, Stephen Hedges, Clive Hemp, Lawrence Hourahane, the late David Irving, John Jenkins, Alan Jones, Ron Jones, the family of the late Willie Jones, Tony Lewis, Brian and Emma Lile, Gareth Mainwaring, Matthew Maynard, the Mercer family, Douglas Miller, David Morgan, Malcolm Nash, Chris Peregrine, Duncan Pierce, the late Jim Pleass, the family of the late Arthur Porter, the late Don Shepherd, Richard Stevens, Richard Thomas, the Turnbull family, Peter Walker, Ossie Wheatley and the Wooller family.

Thanks also to a number of librarians in Swansea and Cardiff, as well as staff at the National Library of Wales in Aberystwyth and the South Wales Miners Institute whose collection is now housed at Swansea University. Other images have been made available from the Glamorgan CCC Archives and Swansea RFC, whilst lastly - but by no means least, thanks to Scott Reeves for acting as proof-reader, and also to the staff at City Press in Leeds for producing such a handsome product.

Andrew Hignell

Index